"*From Tablet to Table* speaks to the heart of God's purpose for humankind—namely, relationships. First, that we will commune with God Himself; and second, with one another. There is no better place to build relationships than at the table with good food and great conversation. *From Tablet to Table* is a great read for those who want to develop their friendship with God and other people."

GERARD LONG
Executive Director, Alpha USA

"Oh, this is a must-read for anyone who, like me, longs for the table to return to the center of our family lives—and the center, indeed, of our faith and practices. Len Sweet is singing a song I love, and he's doing it with intelligence and passion."

SHAUNA NIEQUIST
Author of *Bread and Wine*, shaunaniequist.com

"The table is a recurring biblical theme that Len Sweet engages deeply in *From Tablet to Table*. That's Len's way—he makes us think through signs, stories, and symbols—and he has done so again here. This book will make you think and will stretch your thinking, in classic Sweet fashion. I'll see you at the table."

ED STETZER
President of Lifeway Research, edstetzer.com

"Leonard Sweet is among the few Christian writers of our time whose every work should be carefully read. In this new offering, Sweet reframes the Scriptures from a static tablet of ink to a full menu of spiritual food for the human soul and spirit. This is an engaging study on the meaning of 'the table' throughout Scripture and on how it applies to every hungry and thirsty heart today."

FRANK VIOLA
Bestselling author, speaker, and blogger, frankviola.org

"In our fast-paced/fast-food/ramen-noodle/instant/ disposable-ideas culture, isn't it dreamy to find that our longing for 'something more' isn't a coding error but a spiritual hardwiring? Len Sweet calls us to return to the elemental fundamentals: a table, a meal, a conversation, a conversion. He brings his unique gumbo of narrative/ metaphor/humor/observation/relationship and draws us into new observances of ancient truths. If you're looking for something tasty to sink your teeth into, start here. Len has word-chef'd a soul-savory delight."

ANITA RENFROE
Comedian, anitarenfroe.com

"Len Sweet has always had one of the most fertile minds of the people I know. In this book, he continues in this Sweet tradition by adding lots of spice to our dulled imaginations as well as calling us to party for the sake of the gospel. What's not to like?"

ALAN HIRSCH
Founder of Future Travelers and of Forge Mission Training Network, alanhirsch.org

"With his reflections on the Lord's table and the dinner table as central for Life and life, Len Sweet draws together heaven and earth in a celebration of the ongoing relationships of love. This is a splendid theology to live by."

LUCI SHAW
Author of *Adventure of Ascent: Field Notes from a Lifelong Journey,* lucishaw.com

"Leonard Sweet is right when he says that if we brought back the table as a sacred object of furniture in every home, church, and community, it would change the world for the better. This small treatise on eating invites readers to think differently and more intentionally about something we do multiple times a day."

LISA GRAHAM McMINN
Author of *Walking Gently on the Earth*

FROM tablet TO table

Where community is found and identity is formed

LEONARD SWEET

NAVPRESS

*A NavPress resource published in alliance
with Tyndale House Publishers, Inc.*

NAVPRESS ●®

NavPress is the publishing ministry of The Navigators, an international Christian organization and leader in personal spiritual development. NavPress is committed to helping people grow spiritually and enjoy lives of meaning and hope through personal and group resources that are biblically rooted, culturally relevant, and highly practical.

For more information, visit www.NavPress.com.

For Gloria and Bill Gaither
Two Master Setters of the Table

CONTENTS

Acknowledgments *xi*

Introduction: Bring Back the Table *1*

PART I: **Table It**

ONE: Every Story I Know Best I Learned
from a Flannelgraph *23*

TWO: "Thou Preparest a Table Before Me" *43*

THREE: Jesus, the Messiah of the
Open Table *61*

PART II: **Life's Three Tables**

FOUR: Setting the Table at Home *77*

FIVE: Setting the Table at Church *107*

SIX: Setting the Table in the World *137*

Conclusion *161*

Notes *165*

About the Author *173*

ACKNOWLEDGMENTS

Every book I write is a rock thrown into the water. I heave and trust heaven, hoping that God will create a wave of beauty, truth, and goodness, a wave that rolls on and on, reaching out to the ends of the earth and deep into the spirit of humanity. I am here because of waves from rocks hurled into the ocean by ancestors both biological and theological, some of whose names I know and celebrate, some of whose names I will know only in eternity. The greatest wave comes from the rock Christ threw with his life long ago, the Wave that shook the world like a tsunami shakes a shore.

I am not the first to find the table a fertile metaphor. Without the surgical skills of David Zimmerman, my editor on this project, this book would have died on the table. Whatever circumstances and challenges arose while I was writing this book, Lori Wagner was adept at turning the tables so that it resulted in my advantage, not my disadvantage. My friend Chuck Fromm, and his right arm and left brain Suzie Stablein, are gracious in tabling things in their own lives to deal with my entreaties and importunities. Brett Blair keeps my shortcomings under the table as we conspire to improve the art and craft of preaching.

Thank you also to my doctoral cohorts at George Fox Evangelical Seminary, who heard me talk out loud about many of these thoughts, and who talked back more often than not: Chrysanne Timm, Scott Scrivner, Mitchel Diemer, Eric Petersen, Mark Griffith, Phillip Faig, Matt Edwards, Hambric Brooks, Mark Merrill, Mark Nalepa, Derrick Chan, Mark Chironna, Amm David, Jorge Finlay, and Greg Bratland.

Completion of this book was not made possible by grants from any foundation or learned society or confederacy of funding. Rather, Don Pape believed in this book enough to leave money on the table. When my life's water-table level went down, my family kept me from trouble and managed to find ways to replenish the supply. Being in the presence of Thane, Soren, and Egil are the highwater marks of my life. Elizabeth has been a fundamentalist table setter, even when it was easier to herd cats than to herd kids to the table. The table is her love language, and this book is really the life lessons of her table turned into a tablet.

This book grew from a sermon I first preached at the One Project in Seattle, which I attended with my son Thane at the invitation of Japheth Oliver. I then preached the sermon at the Family Fest in Gatlinburg, Tennessee, at the invitation of Bill and Gloria Gaither. No one has done more to spread a sumptuous table for the church in the past fifty years than Gloria and Bill. In fact, Gloria may just be one of the church's best living theologians. It is to these two master setters of the table in the home, the church, and the world that I dedicate this book.

Leonard Sweet
Orcas Island
Labor Day weekend, 2014

BRING BACK THE TABLE

— ❧ —

You must sit down, says Love, and taste my meat:
So I did sit and eat.
GEORGE HERBERT, "LOVE (III)"

WHEN ANY SPECIES UNDERGOES a reproduction crisis, a name is given it: "endangered." Arguably Christianity has entered such a crisis; our inability to reproduce the faith is the number one problem facing our families and churches today. Christianity in the West has become a sterile, exhausted religion, its power to tell us fresh things about God and life expended in lifeless repetition, imprisoned conventionality, and predictable pastiche. The result is a failure to offer a viable response to the challenges facing the world we're in.

The dominant means of addressing the church's

reproduction crisis has been to devise new method-ologies and strategies for how we do church. This is a misdiagnosis of the problem, however, and without the right diagnosis of the disease, a cure is difficult. Or to put it differently, a category mistake is a catastrophic mistake. And our condition is now catastrophic.

Christianity in the West is suffering from an identity crisis. Instead of finding our identity in Jesus, we have tried to build an alternative identity on a Christian worldview, on biblical values, or on Christian prin-ciples, as though these are the cure-alls for our dete-riorating faith and declining condition. But none of these salve our fear and confusion about who we are and help us to feel joyful and secure in our lives and in a challenging world. None of our "silver bullets" or "golden hammers" can replace what we have lost.

But there is one thing that would dramatically change the world we live in and help return us to our rootedness in Christ: Bring back the table! If we were to make the table the most sacred object of furniture in every home, in every church, in every community, our faith would quickly regain its power, and our world would quickly become a better place. The table is the place where identity is born—the place where the story of our lives is retold, re-minded, and relived.

Humans are wired for story. We become our stories. When we go in search of our identity, we don't look for values or principles or worldviews; we look for fireworks in the sky, synapses that cause our cells to fire together and wire together. Story and image are the protons and neutrons swirling in the cells of our self-concept. At the subcellular level, we don't crave a tablet full of values and principles and props; at the core of who we are, we crave a *narraphor* (a story made with metaphors that help us understand the world, ourselves, and God better).

Given that our culture's primal, primary language of identity is narraphor, our families and churches ought to be flourishing! But something is missing from our lives—something that nourishes us with the narraphors that build our identity and stabilize our relationships. We know that families are defined by the stories they generate, by the stories they remember together over and over. Christian families are defined by the Story of

Jesus and God's relationship to humanity throughout history. And this story of our identity as a Christian people is relayed through the narraphors we tell ourselves, our children, and our grandchildren around the table generation after generation. Narraphors are the lingua franca of the Christian faith. They are our "table talk." But modern Christianity has become more "modern" than Christian, having sold out to a fast-paced, word-based, verse-backed, principles-driven template for truth, a handy little tablet of rules and regulations.

The thing is, truth is not a template. Truth is a person. And our relationship with Jesus—the Way, the Truth, and the Life—happens when narraphors are passed around the table.

Stories build our identity as a person and as a people. In twenty-first-century lingo, they are the food—our "hardware," if you will. And the server, the platform, is the table.

The story of Christianity didn't take shape behind pulpits or on altars or in books. No, the story of Christianity takes shape around tables, as people face one another as equals, telling stories, sharing memories, enjoying food with one another.

THE FOODIE BIBLE

Someone once challenged me: "I bet I can tell you the whole Old Testament and New Testament in six sentences—three for each."

"You're on!" I said.

He started with the Old Testament: "'They tried to kill us. We survived. Let's eat!'"

My friend went on. "Now here's the New Testament in three sentences: 'I love you! I forgive you! Let's eat!'"

Jean Leclerc offers the best definition of the gospel you'll ever hear: "Jesus ate good food with bad people." This was so accurate a description of Jesus that someone in his day composed a satirical jingle about him that went viral: He was "a glutton and a drunkard, a friend of tax collectors and sinners" (Matthew 11:19). Jesus' dining experiences became a lifestyle around which he formed a school of disciples, such that John's account of the Cana wedding suggests that the wine didn't run out until Jesus and the disciples arrived.

As much as Jesus loved food, people always came first. Sometimes he got so preoccupied with people that he forgot to eat (Mark 3:20, 31; John 4:31). But the point remains the same. Jesus was killed because of his table talk and his table manners—the stories he told and the people he ate with.[1] Jesus and table so went together that the Pharisees used a table to try to trap him (Luke 14:1-24). Food is a reference point for Jesus even when he is not eating (see, for example, John 4:32). It was the table that shaped early Christian worship—the Last Supper and the post-Resurrection meals Jesus shared with his disciples. The infant Jesus is laid in a manger, from which the animals were fed; there is a table at the stable. At the very beginning of his post-Resurrection ministry, Jesus suddenly appears in front of his disciples and asks, "Got anything to eat?" (John 21:5).

Food is the building block of our Christian faith. We are part of a gourmet gospel that defines itself in terms of food and table. Yet we find ourselves at a juncture in history where we have lost the table and reduced our "food" to non-foods. Instead of setting another plate at the table and passing the food, we pass another program or pass another resolution or pass another law.

The Pharisees lived by laws, rules, and exclusions. Jesus showed us how to live by love, grace, and inclusion. At the table we don't just feed people; we build relationships—stories and memories. We associate people with the stories we hear of them and the memories we have of them, especially sensory memories: the sounds, tastes, smells, textures, and pictures of them. These are the stuff of metaphors and narraphors.

When I want to tell my kids about the grandfather they never met but am at a loss for words, I get out some graham crackers, serve them some cheesecake, and tell them about the cherry cheesecake their Grandpa Sweet made from graham cracker crust, Philadelphia cream cheese, and Del Monte canned cherries. In so doing, I am enculturating them into the Sweet family; I am connecting the dots between their stories, his, and mine.

If we really want to learn someone's story, sitting down at the table and breaking bread together is the best way to start. First dates almost always involve a meal. As many business deals are sealed over dessert as over desktops. As we sit and eat together, we don't just pass food around; fellow diners pass bits of themselves back and forth as well, exchanging tales as well as condiments. I like any vegetable stir-fried. I like my chicken deep-fried. I like my table story-fied.

At the table, where food and stories are passed from one person to another and one generation to another, is where each of us learns who we are, where we come from, what we can be, to whom we belong, and to what we are called. When I spread apple butter on a biscuit, I am back at my Gramma's table, eating her daily baked biscuits with Granddad's apple butter, straight from his copper apple-butter kettle. Some of my most cherished possessions and among the most beautiful items in my home, my mother's Bibles were bound to become battered and dog-eared, their covers blotched with coffee stains and their pages crumpled from teardrops, with all sorts of things falling from their pages. When I read from one of them, I am not necessarily reading the way she read, but because of what that book and its history represents, I am reading the Story with her voice, and with the same thrill and exhilaration as she had when she read it.

The best in film criticism sends you excitedly back to the films. The best in biblical criticism should send you excitedly back to the Bible, not to start another critique but to reenter the story on a wider and deeper level of comprehension.

THE "FAMILY" TABLE

An untabled faith is an unstable faith. A neglect of the table in our churches is echoed in our families and our communities. In his book *Cooked* Michael Pollan shows that meals eaten out are almost always less healthy than foods cooked in; homemade foods generally have lower fat, salt, and caloric content.[2] And yet we are eating out more and more, eating in less and less. We eat one in every five meals in our car. One in four of us eat at least one fast-food meal every single day. US households spend roughly the same amount per week on fast food as on groceries.[3] Sixty years ago, the average dinnertime was ninety minutes; today it is less than twelve minutes.[4] And that's when we do eat dinner together, which is less and less frequently. The majority of US families report eating a single meal together less than five days a week. And even then our "dinners together" are mostly in front of the TV.

No wonder the average parent spends only 38.5 minutes per week in meaningful conversation with their children.[5] We are losing the table.

This was brought home recently to the Sweet family when one of my kids invited a friend (let's call him "Horace") to spend some days with us over the summer. After the friend left, I commented that Horace seemed somewhat uneasy during his stay in our home. "Was anything wrong?" I asked.

"He did feel a little uncomfortable," my daughter Soren offered.

"Was it something we did?" I asked.

"Sort of," Soren answered. "He said that he has never eaten with his family at a table, and so he wasn't sure how to act or what to do."

A Christian teenager, attending a Christian college, had never eaten a home-cooked meal at a family table.

The media can be both a thermometer registering and a thermostat regulating the temperament of our culture. And much of our culture today reveals fragmented families with busy, out-of-the-box lives that don't conform to what is now considered "traditional" mealtimes. Yet while shows like *Modern Family* portray families that never eat together at the table, an increasing number of shows, such as *Duck Dynasty* and *Blue Bloods*, prominently feature family dinners, including prayers over meals and story sharing. It seems there is a craving for more intimacy in our lives and relationships. And if we can't get it in our homes, we'll at least watch it on TV.

Our culture is hungry for table time. And in this respect, popular culture is right in step with findings in socio-science that advocate for table gatherings. In fact, when sociologist Cody C. Delistraty culled the most recent scientific literature for *Atlantic Monthly*, he discovered proof that the loss of the table has had "quantifiable negative effects both physically and psychologically" on our families and our kids.[6] Here's what he found:

- The #1 factor for parents raising kids who are drug-free, healthy, intelligent, kind human beings? "Frequent family dinners."[7]
- The #1 shaper of vocabulary in younger children, even more than any other family event, including play? "Frequent family dinners."[8]
- The #1 predictor of future academic success for elementary-age children? "Frequent family dinners."
- One of the best safeguards against childhood obesity? "Eating meals together."[9]
- The best prescription to prevent eating disorders among adolescent girls? "Frequent family dinners" that exude a "positive atmosphere."[10]
- The variable most associated with lower incidence of depressive and suicidal thoughts among eleven- to eighteen-year-olds? "Frequent family dinners."[11]

If you want kids with "fewer emotional and behavioral problems, greater emotional well-being, more trusting and helpful behaviors towards others and higher life satisfaction," then you need "more frequent family dinners."[12] In short, better to eat toast and jam together than ham tetrazzini alone. Better to eat simply together than eat haute cuisine alone.[13] In the memories we make and recall, in the stories we tell and retell, in the family recipes we eat and repeat, there are things we learn at the family table we don't learn anywhere else. There is a reason Jesus made eating a sacrament.

But what does it mean to set a "family table"? Jesus defined family differently than the way we've viewed it or the way his contemporaries understood it. Jesus must have scandalized more than Nazareth by not being married. As a Jewish man, and especially a rabbi, you had a duty to God, to your ancestors, and to your family to marry and reproduce. Later rabbis put it bluntly: "Seven things are condemned in heaven, and the first of these is a man without a woman." Far from being a nuclear family advocate, Jesus turned away from his extended biological family, retained his singleness, and claimed instead a discipleship family that included all kinds of people from all walks of life.

Jesus ate all kinds of food around all kinds of tables in all kinds of places with all kinds of people. To be a disciple of Jesus (then and now) is to love to eat, no matter what Jesus cooks and no matter where he sets the table.

Jesus redefined what it means to "be family," just as he redefined what it means to "break bread" together at table. When Jesus fed five thousand people on a hillside, all of them became his "family" and the hillside became his "table." When he cooked along the shore after his resurrection, Jesus' disciples became his family, and some stones around a fire his table. Jesus ate the Passover meal in the Upper Room not with his biological family but with his new family: his male and female disciples. When Jesus said, "Do this in remembrance of me," he was really saying, "Do table in remembrance of me." Whoever "does table" where the Jesus story is remembered is part of the Jesus family.

Eating "in" for Jesus meant more about being in relationship with God and others than inside a specified building. You can eat out and still have a family table. You can eat in and have no table at all. For some, rice and beans or a Big Mac can be a sacred feast if shared together in the spirit of Jesus. For others, the best cooked family meal can be a burdensome offering to grumbling family members.[14]

Jesus' family includes marrieds, singles, widows, orphans, lepers, sinners, even animals. After all, Jesus' bassinet at birth was a food trough for beasts. If you live alone and your pets join you for food, you are sharing your table with your family. If you share a meal out with friends where stories are shared and love is honored, you have redefined family Jesus-style. Whether in church, home, or community, the table you set defines your "family" identity, as long as Jesus is present.

When Jesus reclines at the table with his disciples in the Upper Room triclinium, he warns "woe" to those who don't continue his table and those who sit at table and betray (Luke 22:21-23). A betrayal by one who breaks bread at table is far worse than any anonymous backstabber. The more intimate your relationship, the deeper the cut. The table is a place of intimacy, and those who feast at Jesus' table become family together in a new kind of relationship—one that obliterates dissension, walls, bloodlines, and divisions.

For Jesus the home is not what defines the table; the

table is what defines the home. Whether a single, working mom or an elderly man in a nursing home; whether a four-year-old child or a teenage athlete; whether a married couple or a homeless woman with her dog: We are all invited to Jesus' table and into Jesus' family.

One of our best descriptions of a "blended" family might be when university students gather. In the university of days past, in the manor building was a great hall, a multipurpose room primarily used for long dining tables and that featured pointed-arch cathedral ceilings which, like the cathedral itself, put humans in their place and scaled them appropriately to the divine. There was a time when students would sit at long tables in these halls to have their meals and to be inducted into the long-standing rituals and rhythms that make someone "an Oxford man" or "an Oxford woman." Several times a week, there were three-course evening meals that required a formal dress code of gowns and other unique garb.

The contrast between these table traditions of the past and the current collegiate "mess halls" couldn't be sharper. The modern "great rooms" found in today's student commons are also multipurpose rooms that often feature arched ceilings, but they are architecturally designed to make humans feel larger than life. The rooms have built-in hearths around which people sit, and screens with a bar separate the "great room" from the kitchen or other all-purpose rooms of the commons. But wherever you look, there is no table in sight. And the adjoining cafeterias are chaotic rambling spaces with various drop-by stations catering to diverse ethnic and eating preferences without any common menu or common rituals of community.

And then there are online universities, where your entire learning is conducted on a tablet with no face-to-face table time at all. True online learning is peer-to-peer distributed tablet learning *and* face-to-face immersive table learning, built around a monastic model of community that eats together, worships together, prays together, sings together, lives together, and learns together.

The table is necessarily communal. And for Christians, there is a Trinitarian component to the table. Even when only two are gathered together, three are always present. Wherever we break bread together, Jesus is always at the table. And we are to re-member him, bring him to life in every heart. Because the life of your table becomes the preeminent art of your life. You "become" a disciple to the Master Artist through your time spent together at Jesus' table.

THE HEAD OF THE TABLE

The first word God speaks to human beings in the Bible—God's very first commandment—is "Eat freely" (Genesis 2:16, NASB). The last words out of God's mouth in the Bible—his final command? "Drink freely" (see Revelation 22:17). These bookends to the Bible are reflective of the whole of the Scriptures: Everything in between these two commands is a table, and on that table is served a life-course meal, where we feast in our hearts with thanksgiving on the very Bread of Life and the Cup of Salvation: Jesus the Christ.

At the table, sitting together, facing each other, talking to each other—good food, good conversation, good laughs, good stories—we *learn* the good news of the God who eats good food with bad people. There is nothing else like it in the world. To bring back the vigor to Christianity, to reverse the church's attrition rate, we must bring back the table. The most important thing anyone can do to strengthen our families and reproduce the faith in our kids is to bring back the table. The most important thing anyone can do to change our world for the better is to bring back the table—with Jesus seated at his rightful place.

The king of Scotland invited a local warlord to a banquet he was having at one of his castles. The king wasn't getting along with this warlord, who went by the title "Lord of the Isles," so to showcase his sovereignty, the king seated him at one of the lowly places, far from the king's table. During the meal, the king sent one of his servants to check and make sure that the Lord of the Isles knew that he was in one of the lowly places.

The Lord of the Isles said to the servant, "Go back to your king and tell him that wherever the Lord of the Isles sits, there is the head of the table!"

Wherever Jesus sits, there is the head of the table. And wherever Jesus sits, he has saved you a place.

When your best friend shuts the door in your face,
*   Jesus pulls the chair out for you at his table.*
When everyone else leaves the room,
*   Jesus saves a place for you at his table.*
When everybody fails you,
*   Jesus takes you in at his table.*
When everything in life fails you,
*   Jesus has reserved a special place at his table just*
*   for you.*
When your kids want nothing more to do with you,
*   Jesus wants nothing more than for you to sit down*
*   at his table.*
When your employer wants nothing more to do with
*   you,*
*   Jesus puts you at the head of his table.*

PART I

ONE

EVERY STORY I KNOW BEST I LEARNED FROM A FLANNELGRAPH

A Well-Storied Faith

— ⚕ —

Wisdom . . . has prepared her meat and mixed her wine;
she has also set her table.

PROVERBS 9:1-2

HAVE YOU EVER SAID something you wish you could take back? I've certainly written some things I wish I could take back. One of these mea culpas is a mocking of certain people I have tardily come to honor and celebrate.

In one of my early books, I wrote about how the church finds itself in a digital, electronic culture with computer-savvy kids. Yet our churches are still trying to teach the Bible through flannelgraphs, chalk talks, and chalk artists. I made sport of those people and their ministries.

Now I am so repentant, so embarrassed I ever said such a thing. Every time I meet someone who uses flannelgraphs, I kneel down in front of them and beg, "Please forgive me. I'm so sorry for what I've done. I'm grateful to God for you."

Why the turnaround? Every story I know best I learned from a flannelgraph.

I'm a slow learner about some things, and it took me too long to realize this. For much of my life I have unknowingly suffered from a serious and stealthy illness: versitis.[1]

No, not "bursitis." "Versitis."

What is "versitis," you ask? A burglar broke into a home late one night while a couple was sleeping upstairs. The woman of the house, a Christian who knew her Bible, came to the head of the stairs, saw the shadow of the burglar in the living room, and shouted out, "Acts 2:38!"

That's the verse where Peter tells the crowd, "Repent!"

Immediately the burglar fell to the floor, his hands over his head. He stayed there motionless until the police arrived and took him away.

As he got into the car, the cop said, "So it was Scripture that got you to give up?"

"What? That wasn't Scripture. She yelled she had an axe and two .38s."

From my childhood I have accessed the Bible through the template of books (66), chapters (1,189), and verses (31,103). The problem is that this template is alien to the material. The Bible wasn't written numerically. The Bible was written narratively, metaphorically, in stories and poems and songs and letters and memoirs and autobiographies and dreamscapes. The original template of the Bible is not numbers; it's *narraphors*.[2]

I started learning the chapter-and-verse template as early as my nursery days, through the church's "farm system," a training regimen made up of Sunday school pins, Upper Room certificates, "sword drills" in youth group, college "mission bingos," N. A. Woychuk's Bible Memory Association prizes, and Awana "jewels." This training regimen is systematically being dismantled, however, as more and more resources are being diverted from the farm system to preserve the bureaucracy's factory system. Hence our children's increasing biblical illiteracy, even of the alien template, not to mention their disconnect from the ritual life of the church.

Because the farm system was still vibrant as I grew up in the church, I entered college well-versed in the Bible. At least I thought so. It wasn't until well into my ministry that I realized that, while I had memorized hundreds of Bible verses, I had never memorized a Bible story. Not one. In other words, what I had learned "by heart" was not the story, but the verses. I had "hidden . . . in my heart" (Psalm 119:11) only the parts, not the whole.

When I began itemizing what stories I knew best (Daniel in the Lions' Den, David and Goliath, Jonah and the Whale, Noah and the Flood, the Woman at the Well, the Good Samaritan, the Prodigal Son, the Feeding of the Five Thousand), it suddenly hit me: I had learned all these from flannelgraphs at vacation Bible school, chalk talks at Sunday school, gospel songs at camp meetings, chalk artists at summer camps. If it had not been for the narraphorical teaching of the flannelgraph, I would have a worse case of versitis than I do.

THE GREATEST STORY NEVER TOLD

How bad is our versitis? In my public speaking, I often showcase the greatness of Jesus' communication skills by probing how he masterfully weaves a story around a metaphor, and then declaring, somewhat sarcastically, "This is *not* a Jesus method of communication: 'Here are the seven habits of highly effective discipleship.'" I can always count on a substantial number of people immediately bowing their heads, programmed by this alien template to write down the seven habits I had just said Jesus did *not* give us. Similarly, I have given entire sermons exploring a biblical story in depth, only to have someone come up to me and say, "Missed our having a text this morning." When a Jesus story only counts when it's broken down by the numbers, it is time to be averse to verse. It is versus-verses time.

You can test the severity of your own versitis by a little experiment. Can you recite from memory the most famous Bible verse, John 3:16, "the gospel in a nutshell"? I bet you can recite it perfectly. Now recite John 3:15. No? John 3:14? How about John 3:17? What story is this verse a part of? Because of our versitis, the Bible is too often stripped of story and mined for minutiae; it becomes not "the greatest story ever told" but the greatest story *never* told, or *half*-told.[3]

Don't feel bad. I too was once a Nicodemite. I still am in some ways.

Nicodemus—Jesus' conversation partner in the flannelgraph version of John 3:16 (encompassing John 3:1-21)—is the patron saint of all of us suffering from versitis, as well as all left-brained people. Nick-by-Nite comes to Jesus with a left-brained approach about how to enter the kingdom, and when Jesus tells him he must be born again, he responds, "How can someone be born twice?" And Jesus responds with a right-brained metaphor: "You must be born again of water and of the Spirit." This "ruler of the Jews" interpreted Jesus literally, and mocked Jesus' metaphor:

"Must I enter my mother's womb a second time and be born?" Nicodemus met the law, and the law lost. Nicodemus could understand truth as text, as words, as laws, as left-brain logic. But Nicodemus could not process Jesus' right-brained imagery and poetry of being "born again."

How many Nicodemites are there in every corner of Christianity whose versitis has caused them to be more committed to words than to the Word Made Flesh? How many have made a religion of words and lost sight of God's Image-Made-Story?[4] Jesus was trying to show Nicodemus how crippling versitis can be. A faith that doesn't know what a metaphor is can't sustain us, nor can it grasp who God is and how God relates to us. In the fourth century, for example, the Arians read the Nicene Creed literally, believing that Jesus was literally "begotten" by the Father in the same way we are "begotten" by our parents. They never did get the "begotten" metaphor. They could only think literally, and by beating down and banishing the metaphor, they knocked the stuffing out of an inspired, imaginative truth.

Meaning in life is not found from reducing things into smaller categories and making finer distinctions. Meaning in life is found in putting things together; connecting the dots; and getting the "big picture," which can be told in narrative and metaphor.

You furnish the pictures. I'll furnish the war.
newspaper tycoon William Randolph Hearst (1863–1951)

YOUR BRAIN ON STORY

One of the most exciting conversations today is taking place at the intersection of theology and brain science; it is the most fertile and generative conversation going. We have learned more about the brain (and by extension, us) in the last twenty years than in all of previous history. For example, the human brain processes forty thoughts every second. How? Its complex circuitry of 100 billion neurons make 100 trillion connections. In other words, you can never only do one thing.[5] Even though much of this research treats the brain as a computer, which is vulnerable to reductionist assumptions,[6] the thrust of the research suggests that when it comes to the human brain, the whole is greater than the sum of its parts. With so many connections being made at such a rapid pace, the brain assumes a grand narrative within which everything else fits. In this way brain science and cognitive studies are telling us about the built-in human need for religion: The human brain, it appears, is hardwired for God, the Prime Mover. We were made for a relationship with our Maker.

We are also learning from cognitive science and its ancillary disciplines[7] that words come last. Behind every word there is a backstory, which is based on a root metaphor. The right brain is primal and primary, as we prove every time we dream in wordless images and cinematic stories. To be human is to possess, and live out of, a store of stories.

Paul Ricoeur, in a series of revolutionary studies, demonstrated that *mythos* (the defining stories of a culture) and *mimésis* (the culture's underlying understanding of reality) are two features of the same process. A narrative is the extension of a metaphor;

a metaphor is an extract of narrative. The three "transcendentals of being"—beauty, truth, goodness—Ricoeur describes as "metaphorical acts": After every disaster, the first thing survivors look for amid the rubble is not their diamonds, jewelry, or even safes. They look for their pictures, the images that tell the stories of their lives.

Narraphor precedes principles, and stories and images are the crucibles of thought. Metaphors are the primary path to perceive reality, including the reality of God. To testify to truth is not to versify but to storify.

Lunch will keep us together.

Neil Sedaka

GATHERING AROUND THE STORY

The church used to have "story time," or "testimony time." The early Methodists called this practice a "love feast," and it featured food and a table.

The best place to tell a story is at a table. When you tell a story, you are transferring your experiences directly to the brains of those listening; they feel what you feel, think what you think, smell what you smell. You are teleporting your story to their brain. Research on the brain activity of storytellers demonstrates that the brain patterns of their audience can start to mimic their own.[8] Professional storytellers tell of getting an audience in a "story trance"; people so come under the spell of a story that they start breathing together, nodding their heads in unison, gasping in unison, smiling in unison, moving eyes in unison. It's almost as if they are reenacting the story in real time. Could this be what it means to "have the same mindset as Christ Jesus" (Philippians 2:5)? By the telling and retelling of the Jesus story, God syncs our mind with Christ.

It is important for each one of us to tell our story and hear each other's story. Every person is a story wrapped in skin. Moreover, everyone lives multistoried lives; as our lives intersect, so do our stories, and new stories splinter out from each encounter. As the old country song put it, "We live in a two-story house. / She's got her story and I've got mine." But the ultimate story is the Jesus story of what God has done in the past, is doing in the present, and will do in the future. It's that story that binds all our stories together.

What we need more than anything else is not more storybooks but more storypeople—people who together participate in the bigger story being told by Jesus. We need to tell a bigger story with our life than the story of ourselves. Our stories should point not just to ourselves but to Christ. If storytelling is brain-syncing, then telling God's story is God-syncing. As we gather around the table, we learn to live well-storied lives, and to connect our story to God's story.

Beyond God-syncing, as storytellers we need to engage in world-syncing. Every company that understands its audience is reorganizing itself not around the product it sells but around its *story*, its core identity in relation to its context. In a story-driven world, the one with the best story wins.

A proposition is a picture of reality.
A proposition is a model of reality as we imagine it.
Ludwig Wittgenstein

THE WAY OF THE TABLE

When we all speak the same language, fewer words are necessary. When we don't speak the same language, more words are required. One of the reasons for the "wordiness" of the church at this point in its history is that we no longer speak the vernacular of the culture. This culture speaks the language of narraphor. Maybe it's time we learned the vernacular of the culture we're in. People are now organizing their lives by adding the best chapters they can to their life story. A sense of self is no longer about "worldviews" or "values clarification" or "leadership principles." It's all about dramatizing and monumentalizing one's life story.

The stories and images Jesus gave us, on the other hand, lift our stories into his. The narraphors of Jesus constitute a universal language with many dialects, each one collapsing the distance between ourselves and the people who came before us, each one connecting ourselves to the people who will come after us. Jesus' narraphors are monumental in and of themselves; they point to the epic story of God and God's world; they are worth living for and dying for.

"If the world could write by itself," the Russian short-story writer Isaak Babel mused, "it would write like Tolstoy." I say, if creation could speak, it would speak like Jesus. Christians believe that creation does speak. All the earth tells its story in the Jesus story. Every stone sings out the stories of Jesus. And so do we. The stories of Jesus, as monumental as they are, are not heroic legends or tales of the heavens. They are ordinary stories of ordinary people in ordinary places doing ordinary things like fishing, tilling fields, and setting tables, but in an extraordinary way.

The ideal place to learn the Jesus stories and the Jesus soundtrack is at the table. Throughout the ages, all over the world, people gather together at a meal in order to get to know each other. If we really want to learn someone's story, sitting down at the table, breaking bread together, is the best way to start. As we sit and eat together, we don't just pass food around; fellow diners pass bits of themselves back and forth as well, exchanging tales as well as condiments. What's the mortar to build community? The grout of grace that is ladled out at mealtime.

A creed is an ossified metaphor.

Elbert Hubbard

STARVING WITH FOOD IN SIGHT

A poor man had wanted to go on a cruise all his life. As a youth he had seen an advertisement for a luxury cruise and had dreamed ever since of spending a week on a large ocean liner, enjoying fresh sea air and relaxing in a luxurious environment. He saved money for years, carefully counting his pennies, often sacrificing personal needs so he could stretch his resources a little further.

Finally he had enough to purchase a cruise ticket. He went to a travel agent, looked over the cruise brochures, picked out one that was especially attractive, and bought a ticket. He was hardly able to believe he was about to realize his childhood dream.

Knowing he could not afford the kind of elegant food pictured in the brochure, the man planned to bring his own provisions for the week. Accustomed to moderation after years of frugal living, and with his entire savings going to pay for the cruise ticket, the man decided to bring along a week's supply of bread and peanut butter. That was all he could afford.

The first few days of the cruise were thrilling. The man ate peanut butter sandwiches alone in his room each morning and spent the rest of his time relaxing in the sunlight and fresh air, delighted to be aboard ship.

By midweek, however, the man was beginning to notice that he was the only person on board who was not eating luxurious meals. It seemed that every time he sat on the deck or rested in the lounge or stepped outside his cabin, a porter would walk by with a huge meal for someone who had ordered room service.

By the fifth day of the cruise, the man could take it no longer. The peanut butter sandwiches seemed stale and tasteless. He was desperately hungry, and even the fresh air and sunshine had lost their appeal. Finally, he stopped a porter and exclaimed, "Tell me how I might get one of those meals! I'm dying for some decent food, and I'll do anything you say to earn it!"

"Why, sir, don't you have a ticket for this cruise?" the porter asked.

"Certainly," said the man. "But I spent everything I had for that ticket. I have nothing left with which to buy food."

"But sir," said the porter, "didn't you realize? Meals are included in your passage. You may eat as much as you like!"[9]

The person in that parable is me, and you, and all those who suffer from versitis. We are sailing on the "ole ship of Zion" where the very food that can carry us beyond ourselves into genuine union and knowledge of things eternal and divine—stories, symbols, signs, sounds, images—are spread out on the banquet table 24/7, while we barely survive on a peanut butter diet of words and points. We live in poverty when we're entitled to banquet abundance through our boarding ticket, which reads "children of God." The eternal feast begins not later, but here and now.

Some people, afflicted with versitis, get rattled when I suggest they read the Bible less as a document and more as a documentary, less a tablet than a table, less chopped-up verses than one story from Genesis to Revelation. They think that the way of faith is to leave childish things like flannelgraphs behind and to focus their discipleship on the principles, values, and worldviews they can mine out of every little verse. Story time, like snack time, is for kids; they need to bury their heads in the Good Book like good adult Christians. But then I remind them that God gave Ezekiel a scroll of his words and commanded him to eat it (Ezekiel 3:1). The tablet is itself a table—"as sweet as honey," as Ezekiel put it (3:3).

Jewish children learn that the Torah is "sweeter than honey" (Psalm 119:103) on their first day of Hebrew school. In the twelfth century, Jewish children would lick Hebrew letters of the Torah written in honey (our ancestors' equivalent to candy) upon a slab of slate to begin their study. The "sweetness" of a life of learning was reinforced by ingesting the sweetness of God's words. Just as Petrarch routinely kissed a manuscript of Homer to show his reverence and respect, so the table is where we kiss the sweeter-than-honey stories of the Scriptures—the tablet made table.

TWO

"THOU PREPAREST A TABLE BEFORE ME"

Our Identity Condition

— ❧ —

Jesus still visits earth for supper. Or lunch. Or breakfast.
Or brunch. Or afternoon tea. Or . . .

CONRAD GEMPF, *Mealtime Habits of the Messiah*

IF A PROBLEM PERSISTS for generations, it is no longer a crisis. It's a condition. The identity crisis facing
our faith, our families, and our world has prevailed so
long it is now a condition—a condition of shadows
and storms, yielding a world of confusion and conflict,
unruly souls, and unraveling societies.

As both consequence and contributing factor, eating has become not so much a God-designed daily
routine of identity formation as a function, a proce-
dure to ingest the energy we need to keep going, or
a therapy of comfort foods to alleviate our anxieties.

In such a context, to return to the table is to come to our senses, to "taste and see that the LORD is good" (Psalm 34:8).[1] We've been tasteless and senseless (and hence identity-less) for far too long.

The first thing the person walking through shadows and storms is met by is a table:

You prepare a table before me. (PSALM 23:5)

Not a quick bite, or a loaded backpack, or a jam-packed lunch pail. Those walking "through the darkest valley" (v. 4) are promised an unhurried, sit-down meal to eat in peace—even "in the presence of [our] enemies" (v. 5).

Lest you think this mention of food in the midst of trouble is an isolated incident in the Scriptures, recall the beginning of the exodus from Egypt: From the burning bush God speaks to Moses that he wants to deliver them from their identity as slaves in Egypt to "a land flowing with milk and honey" (Exodus 3:8).

To come out of our shadows and storms, first we need to come to the table and sit at the place God has prepared for us.

To come to the table is to discover who God is and who we are. One of the hardest things in life is to wear your own skin. From day one, we are programmed more for repetition than disclosure, or for imitation of what we see rather than revelation of who we are.

To come to the table is to discover your context and find your direction. It was to address her identity that God asked Hagar in the wilderness, "Where have you come from, and where are you going?" (Genesis 16:8). True identity looks both forward and backward at the same time.

To come to the table is to learn to be our real selves—not some construct conceived by someone else, but who God made us to be. Each one of us must choose to be ourselves, but none of us dine alone. We don't sit at the table by ourselves, but are surrounded, encouraged, and sometimes propped up by parents, patrons, partners, pastors, prayers, paraclete—those who we see when we look around the table.

OUR UNTETHERED SELVES

Identity graduates destiny. Who you are determines where you are headed. That's why all the "royal pages" who served as apprentices in the royal palaces of monarchs were scions of nobility. You couldn't be a royal page if you didn't prove your nobility, and the costs of getting your fourteen-year-old child chosen to serve as a page were enormous. Not to mention the fact that a page was on call virtually 24/7. But the access the royal pages got to the king was unparalleled. Pages were often present at hunts, and they would put on picnics for the royal family. But mostly pages helped out at formal dinners, where they hovered in the background appropriately dressed, waiting around until the end to enjoy the scraps.[2] Once having completed their term as a page, they were tightly connected to the royal family; their nobility was secured both in identity and in destiny.

A noble self-identity destined to stand up and stand out is proving ever harder to form, however. Identities on the Internet are by nature unstable.

The questions kids wrestle with today are no longer "What are my unconditional values?" "What family traditions will I uphold?" or "How strong is my faith in times of trouble?" but rather "What should I wear today?" "Who am I?" and "What celebrity should I emulate?" At best we have partial identities, tentative self-definitions, provisional commitments that are susceptible to the next trending topic.[3] Our identity has become so fluid that we are drowning in celebrity fixations, wishy-washy from our consumerist lifestyles and diluted in our discipleship.

One of the most mysterious medical conditions is called "body integrity identity disorder" (BIID). No one knows what causes it. No one even knows whether it's a physical condition or psychological ailment. Some suspect it is a neurological malfunction in body mapping. Whatever the cause, those who suffer from BIID are miserable, out of sorts, and not at home in their bodies—especially not with certain parts of their body (the left leg especially).

BIID-ers plead with doctors to have healthy limbs amputated and replaced with prostheses. Some will self-amputate, presenting surgeons with a fait accompli. Doctors are unwilling to amputate, not because they doubt the effectiveness of the prosthesis or the future "capability" of its recipient; any loss of function would likely be more than compensated for by the patient's enhanced sense of well-being. But it seems wrong to amputate a healthy leg and replace it with a prosthetic.[4]

Body integrity identity disorder is not a bad description of our psychological as well as religious condition. If your sense of selfhood doesn't come from the table, it comes from cultural turntables that broadcast the body across time, space, and knowledge in probationary, not probative, ways.

Lord lift me up, and let me stand
By faith on Canaan's tableland

Johnson Oatman, Jr., "I'm Pressing On the Upward Way"

It is no wonder that our children are increasingly being diagnosed with "DID" (dissociative identity

48

disorder). We try to "find ourselves" in the surrogate spirituality of consumerism, where our identity is externally driven, the outside caving in on the soul. We try to "find ourselves" in the world of celebrityhood, a narrative vehicle for people who are looking for a bigger and better storyline for themselves.

The true path to "finding ourselves," however, is by *losing* ourselves—through inwardly grown and divinely drawn identity formation.[5] Addressing our identity condition begins with us, the confrontation of our "double books," our refusal to accept the reality of the story we find ourselves in.

OUR STORIED IDENTITY

Jesus gave his disciples a "storied identity"—meaning that he framed their identity in the stories he told as he walked about, healed, and taught in ancient Palestine. The stories and metaphors that Jesus reframed hearkened back to God's very creation at the beginning of time, so to be a follower of Jesus means, in some ways, you have to be a Jew first—you have to be in a right relationship with Judaism. Our true identity begins in the Old Testament with the Jewish collective memory, with the people of Israel whose identity was rooted in God's miraculous salvation from slavery in Egypt. Our identity deepens with the New Testament, where Jesus increases the use of narraphors to plumb the depths of our human nature.

But how can we acquire a "storied identity"? We must make the Bible strange again. The world awaits those who can present such a rich gospel that it leaves people spellbound, filled with awe, and desperate to know their inimitable Lord. And where do we tell those stories that build roots and shoots? Around the table—the place where true discipleship is born.

There is no agony like bearing an untold story inside you.
Zora Neale Hurston, Dust Tracks on the Road

I have had people challenge me on bringing up my children without religious choices. "Don't you think you're being a bit imperialistic and colonialist, not letting your children choose what religion they want to follow?"

My answer is, yes, I am being a bit imperialistic and colonialist. But I'm that way about plenty of other things besides religion. I didn't ask my child, "What language would you like to speak?" or "What economic level would you like to live at?" or "What country would you like to be a part of?" These things are circumstantial to our birth. They are stories we are born into. So if you're born in my house, guess what? "As for me and my household, we will serve the LORD" (Joshua 24:15). A child doesn't decide to have toes; she discovers that she has them; this is how a child of mine discovers that he or she is already part of the body of Christ.

Many kids, once they have flown the coop, fail to fledge fully as disciples of Jesus. Almost all Protestant denominations have plummeting retention rates, keeping only 30–50 percent of their kids into adulthood.[6] There are some studies that say the church is losing upwards of 90 percent of its kids.[7] Maybe we could learn some things from religions with higher retention rates.[8]

The Old Order Amish, for example, despite a refusal to evangelize and a particularly stringent form of Christian faith, keep 95 percent of their kids. Elders teach succeeding generations the songs and stories of the faith around the table. Family devotions take place at the table. The table is where the Amish tradition of *Nachfolge*, of "following after" Jesus, is introduced and instilled in the children. Even when an Amish teenager goes on *Rumspringa* ("running around," a period in which some adolescents leave the group to experience life outside the community), their place at the table is still set, three times a day. Some Amish families even put food on their plate in anticipation of their "running around" kids returning to the table.[9] Amish life, in short, revolves around the table, and it's rare for a young person to leave it behind.[10]

Mormon theology is similarly effective in retaining its youth into adulthood. In many ways a theology of the family, Mormonism makes families a first-order priority, emphasizing three things: a formal declaration of the faith, after which kids understand themselves as "heirs of God and co-heirs with Christ" (Romans 8:17, some of the most hopeful words in all of world literature); an intentional process of discipleship and identity formation; and perhaps most importantly, a family mealtime in which parents intentionally seek to "train up a child in the way he should go" (Proverbs 22:6, NIV 1984). Pastor Jon Nielson sees these three practices as essential for retaining children in the faith as they enter adulthood.[11]

Finally, the Jews—who represent a statistically insignificant .00185 percent of the world's population—have had an impact on science, medicine, literature, and the arts well beyond that of any other people group. The steeple of the Museum of the Jewish People in Tel Aviv, Israel, is called "the Pillar of Remembrance," because there one finds testimony to the way the Jewish people have overcome the worst suffering to achieve epic triumphs.[12] The Jews have seven official feasts, but the center of religious life in Judaism was not the massive slaughter of animals to accommodate its feast calendar, but the telling of stories around the table. In fact, the most sacred ritual today in the Jewish religion is the Passover, in which a family gathers at the table and the father serves up a meal that tells the Jewish story.

In the Seder, the story of the Jews' deliverance from slavery in Egypt is told not by the father but by the food. Children are encouraged to question the story, to probe it, even to doubt it. The Story is strong enough, it is assumed, to take on anything you can bring to it. There is a sense that to be a child of the story is not to proclaim final answers but to profess a life story and devote oneself to a lifelong pilgrimage. The story becomes "my story" by my participation in the story and my interrogation of the story. It is thus a requirement of Judaism that you don't just learn the story, but you see yourself in the story. The tagline for the Museum of the Jewish People suggests as much: "You are part of the story."

The Jewish table is a place of fireworks. Ideas that emerge there diffuse, spread, and intermingle, producing energy and sometimes propagating into new ideas. The Jewish table is not hospitable to ego-driven debates; rather, the table encourages logic and inquiry, uncertainty, and the exercise of one's intelligence. It is the rigors of the Jewish table that contributes to the endurance of the Jewish people. The quest for identity demands the questioning of identity.

A Jewish child becomes an adult at age thirteen, when he or she is mitzvahed; by that point the child has an identity based on the story learned at the table. He or she can spend many teenage years confidently exploring the other stories that populate the world, having already honed his or her sense of self. When a Christian child enters the teenage years, by comparsion, too often that child is told, "Now go find yourself."

Of course, the broader culture is eager to storify our kids: "Build your identity on my sneakers!" "See yourself through this singer!" "Discover your best self in these jeans!" Too often we leave our kids to fashion an identity for themselves in the wilderness of these mass-mediated images. But Jesus didn't go to the wilderness to find himself. Jesus went into the wilderness to encounter God. Paul didn't say, "I know who I am." Paul said, "I know whom I have believed" (2 Timothy 1:12). Identities are indigenous, homegrown, not mass-disseminated. They are revealed in a context, not mediated without context. They are reflective of an underlying truth, not born of trends.

It is at the table that tribal identity is formed. Table is where you learn the stories of your ancestors, the stories that shape your future. We often talk about the bar ("son") or bat ("daughter") mitzvah ("commandment") as a Jewish "coming of age" ritual. These are not something you have, however; they are something you become. You become bar mitzvahed. You become bat mitzvahed. To be bar or bat mitzvahed means to have become a son or daughter of the commandment, of the blessing, of the story. As a Jew is bar mitzvahed or bat mitzvahed, so a Christian might be thought of as bar or bat messiahed. We become sons and daughters of the risen and rising Lord, children of the Blessing, offspring of the Story. At the Eucharistic table we partake of the Bread of Life and the Cup of Salvation, and we become messiahed.

TABLE ETHICS

At the table you learn tribal boundaries, the manners and customs of the table. Table boundaries create stable identities. Every table needs to have rituals of what is right and wrong, what is applauded and what is abhorred. Every table has its own mouth tastes and moral tastes.

When we find our identity in Christ, we are introduced to those uniquely Christian table boundaries. They are drawn from the Bible, but they do not come from biblical principles, propositions, or even isolated verses of Scripture. They come from the full-orbed, multi-storied world of the Bible. We are to manifest Christ, not just mimic him. We are to be not imitators but incarnators of Christ.

Of course, we must each find our unique cleft in the Rock of Ages. Without solid ground beneath our feet, we often hit rock bottom. At least I did. And even with a firm foundation, we can go through periods where we mock the ground on which we stand or the rock from whence we were hewn. Christian identity formation is a *process* of soul making that comes through story shaping. Consider the old hymn that advises, "Take time to be holy." It takes time to be holy, and much of that time should be logged at the table, with other Christians, sharing stories and soaking in the Story that Jesus gives us.

There is an old saying, "Fishing isn't just fishing." Similarly, eating isn't just eating. Food connects us to one another while setting us apart, giving us a unique tribal identity. In Jesus' day, Jewish authorities protected their identity by not eating with "sinners" and people of bad repute. But Jesus didn't care about a "holy table" as the religious establishment defined "holy." For Jesus a holy table was one that was open to anyone, a table where all God's children were present.

That "holy table" could be anywhere: in a homeless shelter, in a café, in an online chat room, at a casino—anywhere grace is needed. Jesus didn't keep a *moral* table, he kept a *healing* table. People who sat at table with Jesus didn't see him primarily as a moral teacher but as a healer and friend. For Jesus, the very thing that set his followers apart is what united them as a group:

"Whatever you did for one of the least of these brothers and sisters of mine, you did for me" (Matthew 25:40).

A "holy" church, then, is a "friend-of-sinners" church. Which raises the question: Is your church holy?

HAPPINESS IS FOUND AT TABLE

It's not just a cultural coincidence that throughout the ages, all over the world, people gather together at a meal in order to get to know one another. It's how we really connect with other people. That's why first dates almost always involve a meal. Ask match.com. Or eharmony.com. Or Zoosk.com. Or ChristianMingle.com. Or my favorite: dateafarmer .com. You can't build a relationship without spending time together. You can't get to know someone without talking with them. The best place to spend time together, talking to each other and getting to know one another, is at the table. Relationships are not like mirrors, where everything you see is really about you. Relationships are like meals, where you feed yourself while feeding each other.

Scholar George Myerson has recently written a study of happiness. After 250 pages tracking moments of joy throughout history, he concludes that humans are happiest hanging with friends, gathered around tables with good food and conversation and laughter. If you can get that table out of doors, so the sun can kiss the skin—if as you dine together you can also provide help for others—then, according to Myerson, you've won the lottery of life.[13]

THREE

JESUS, THE MESSIAH OF THE OPEN TABLE

— ❧ —

Taste is made of a host of distastes.

PAUL VALERY

Jesus is the Messiah of the open table. To think about Jesus is to think about food and table.

The story of Jesus is the story of the table. You can't think about Jesus without thinking about the table, its meals and its rituals. In fact, if you are reading the Gospels and you are not getting hungry, you're missing the meat of the Gospels. It's hard to find a story or scene where Jesus is not fingering food, feeding himself or others. When a crowd gathered, Jesus' first concern was their being watered and fed. While John the Baptist found his mission in the austerity of the wilderness, Jesus gladly admitted that he came "eating and drinking" (Matthew 11:19). The Gospels even begin with a table: The Bread of Life was laid in a manger, a feeding trough.

You can have body without spirit, but spirit seeks body; in the Bible, "Spirit" is associated with materiality, relationship, and incarnation—food (especially feeding the hungry), seamless garments (especially clothing the naked), shelter (especially housing the homeless), perfume (especially eau de Jesus). Jesus' mission does not reject the world, as some contemporary worldviews did out of an abhorrence of materiality; Jesus' mission frees the world from all that would vaporize it. For Jesus, knowing how to eat well is key to knowing how to live well.

Jesus was never more original than at the table. In the words of Adam Gopnik, "Jesus ate what he liked where he liked with whom he liked, a table open to all."[1] It was the sheer openness of his table, in fact, that got him killed. For at the table Jesus declared himself Messiah ("anointed" by God) for the wretched of humanity—shepherds, refugees on the run, lepers, and other sinners.

Every culture has discriminated against the physically impaired and kept them from the table. Consider, for example, the graphic little catalog in the Messianic Rule of the Qumran community, dated to the middle of the first century BC:

No man smitten in his flesh, or paralyzed
in his feet or hands, or lame, or blind, or
deaf, or dumb; no old and tottery man
unable to stay still . . . let him not enter
among the congregation for he is smitten.
(1QSa, "The Rule of the Congregation")

Or consider the exclusion rules in Leviticus, datable in its present form to the return of the Jewish leadership from captivity in Babylon (thus after about 538 BC):

No one who has a blemish shall draw near, one
who is blind or lame, or one who has a mutilated
face or a limb too long, or one who has a broken
foot or a broken hand, or a hunchback, or
a dwarf. (See Leviticus 21:16-24.)

Beyond the obvious delinquents, derelicts, and deformed that were kept from the table, the laws of ritual purity kept Torah-observant Jews from dining with Gentiles. It also kept at arm's length Jews whose Torah observance was questionable or negligible ("tax collectors and sinners"). Tax collectors did business with the Roman government every day and thus interacted physically and socially with Gentile culture and traditions. "Sinners" defined any and all who failed to live a pure life—maintaining dietary observances, attending daily prayers, offering Temple sacrifices, avoiding outsiders or the "unclean."

Jesus broke all the dining rules of his day, introducing a whole new set of table manners. He ate on fast days. He ate with dirty hands. He ate with tax collectors. He called a sinner out of a tree and invited himself to his home for dinner. He sipped water at a well out of the bucket of a woman of highly questionable reputation. With no home of his own, Jesus ate as a guest in someone's home every night of his missionary life.

But the most subversive move of all was this: Wherever Jesus dined, he was the guest—and yet he always took on the role of the host. When Jesus showed up for dinner, the menu changed. Instead of simply good food, those around the table received the gift of God's presence and the super-food of faith. It is a gift that still continues at every faithful meal we sit down to today.

It seems also that Jesus always left leftovers. At the Jesus table there was not just enough; there was, as my Appalachian Gramma used to say, an "ample sufficiency." And that ample sufficiency was used to feed the hungry and needy.

The religious establishment was scandalized by Jesus' "party" attitude, and as his dining companions grew ever sketchier, the Pharisees and scribes publicly complained about Jesus' apparent failure to follow proper dietary observances and eating protocols. Jesus addressed head-on the "grumbling" (*diagonguzo*) the Pharisees and scribes leveled against him: "This man welcomes sinners and eats with them" (Luke 15:2). The term *prodechetai* ("welcomes") suggests Jesus did not just "receive" these sinners but had genuine goodwill, even an eager expectation, about their arrival. He was excited to see them and looked forward to his time at table with them.

Jesus responded to the charge of "loose religion" by telling "loose" stories about "loose" people. He even broke custom and pointedly explained the "app" of some of those stories. Three of the stories focus on the lost being found: the "lost sheep," the "lost coin," and the "lost son" (Luke 15). But in other stories Jesus makes it as plain as a pain in the neck how important it is for him that all God's children sit with him and around him at his table.

> When you give a luncheon or dinner, do not
> invite your friends, your brothers or sisters,
> your relatives, or your rich neighbors. . . .
> But when you give a banquet, invite the
> poor, the crippled, the lame, the blind.
> (Luke 14:12-13)

When Jesus performed his first miracle at a wedding feast, he put the sign of joy and feasting over his entire ministry. Water that had been set apart for sacred purposes Jesus turned into wine, thereby erasing any distinction between the sacred and the secular. In so doing Jesus used the table as a gateway drug into the kingdom.

The kingdom of God is not a geographic domain with set boundaries and settled decrees, but a set of relationships in which Christ is sovereign. At the table, Jesus moves us from ideas about life and love to actual living and loving.

Martin Luther was right. Theology is table talk.[2]

Jesus didn't sell the food of his Father. He issued invitations to the table. In fact, Jesus' favorite image for the kingdom of God is a banquet where everyone is sitting around a table.

Not everyone came to these banquets. Not all accepted his invitation. Some mocked his invitation. Some conspired to kill him because of others he had invited.

But whether you accepted or declined Jesus' invitation, there would be a feast (Matthew 22:1-14). You didn't have to come. But Jesus would hold a place for you in case you changed your mind.

DINING DECORUM

Life in the ancient world revolved around meals. Roman banquets, also known as "symposia" (most definitely *not* the staid lectures we think of when we hear this term) were scenes of exquisite excess, the very definition of "conspicuous consumption." Sometimes lasting for ten hours or more, they featured gluttonous amounts of food, course after course of rich delicacies. And the food was just the precursor for the tidal waves of wine and other "entertainment" that would follow. Weddings were when hosts put on the ritz, featuring flamingo tongues, or mullet livers, or swans stuffed with live larks, or any number of other delicacies favored by first-century Roman gourmet Marcus Gavius Apicius.[3]

The saddest feature of these Greco-Roman banquets was the theology behind it. All of this partying was a decoy designed to distract their pantheon of bored and mercurial gods from any meddling or punishment they might want to rain down upon the pathetic, mortal human population. The Romans used

"bread and circuses" not just to keep th
lace happy, but also to keep their unprec
sky-length distance.

Dining in first-century Jewish househol
a bit different. The mandates of Torah tem_ ured the
economic differences between the peasant population
and the educated elite. While the Sanhedrin and other
members of the religious establishment no doubt had
more funds to spend on food, they maintained the
basic diet and mealtime practices that were observed
daily in every Jewish household.

Unlike the Romans, Jewish feast days did not
exist to keep God away but to invite God's presence.
Whether it was a formal "feast day" or the weekly
"Shabbat," the shared meal invoked and invited God's
presence. Indeed, it was the presence of the divine that
made these meals sacred and special.

The upper echelons of Roman society practiced
the "daily decline," which entailed standing for breakfast, sitting for lunch, and reclining for dinner, the
big meal of the day. But the eating posture of Jews
differed. The Essenes at Qumran, for example, had

communal dining rooms where they ate sitting instead of reclining.[4]

Jesus did not reject the Greco-Roman custom of reclining while dining, and there are ample episodes where Jesus reclines at meals[5] and an image of heaven where people "recline at the table in the kingdom of God" (Luke 13:29, NASB). At the last supper there is evidence of reclining as well (John 13:23). And while the Essenes all ate from individual bowls and carefully measured portions meted out to each member of the community, Jesus and his disciples most likely followed the practice of the Greco-Roman world, where diners shared food out of common dishes.[6]

We know Jesus loved bread, figs, and broiled fish, and enjoyed cooking for others. He probably also relished pomegranates, dates, and grapes (all of which were used in the making of wine), as well as honey, olives, lamb, and vinegar. How much fancier the cooking got, we can't be sure. We do know that one reason Bethany was Jesus' favorite place on earth was that he loved Martha's cooking.[7]

The main thing that distinguishes mealtimes with

Jesus, as Conrad Gempf has shown, from the meals of his contemporaries are four verbs.[8] Whether it's the feeding of the five thousand, the Last Supper, or the Emmaus meal, four things take place:

First, Jesus *takes* something.
Second, Jesus *blesses* what he takes.
Third, Jesus *breaks* what he has blessed.
Fourth, Jesus *gives* away what he has broken,
    to be a miracle in the lives of others.

First, *Jesus takes something*. It doesn't matter what it is. No matter how meager or damaged or out-of-touch it is, it comes to life at the touch of God.

Second, *Jesus blesses what he takes*. You never get a blessing for yourself. You get a blessing to bless others. In the words of the black church, "a blessing can't get to you unless it first can go through you." We are blessed to bless.

Third, *Jesus breaks what he has blessed*. The word *company* derives from Latin words *cum* and *pane*, meaning "breaking bread together." *Companion* means "the one who brings the bread along," a community of broken people breaking bread together.[9] Every day I make plans to live forever, but bless everyone I meet that day as having one broken thing in common: the life we soon must lose.

Fourth, *Jesus gives away what is broken.* For Jesus it is not enough to be creative and witty and wise in oneself. Are you the cause of creativity and wit and wisdom in others? Just as we are blessed as we bless, we are fed as we feed. At the table we feed others the Bread of Life to be fed the Bread of Life. The more we give, the more we receive.

Of course, these four verbs become one in Jesus himself, who *is* the Bread, blessed, broken, and bestowed. Some of Jesus' followers thought he came to give bread to them like manna in the desert. The truth was Jesus came to *be* bread for them—and for us.

The Risen One rises when we grasp, bless, break, and give away. The place where we gather; the place where we invite Jesus only to find that he has prepared a table before us; the place where what we bring he takes, blesses, breaks, and bestows on us to be distributed, with confidence that there will be more than enough for the whole world. And when we, as followers of Jesus—as people of the table—take what is presented to us, bless it, break it, and bestow it as a blessing, we emulate our Lord, and the Risen One rises again.

life's three tables

FOUR

SETTING THE TABLE AT HOME

— ❧ —

*[The table is] the raft to ride down the river of
our existence even in the hardest times.*

ADAM GOPNIK, *The Table Comes First*

IF THE TABLE IS A SYMBOL OF everything right about life
and love, "Breakfast Mates" is a symbol of everything
wrong. Everything that is wrong with the world today
is here in this one product.

Introduced by Kellogg's Company in 1998,
Breakfast Mates were a single serving of cereal in a
disposable bowl, a small carton of unrefrigerated milk,
and a plastic spoon—all in one package. (Ralston
Purina had a similar product called Breakfast on the
Run.) "It's for today's busy family," boasted Kellogg's
in a $30 million advertising campaign. It let kids make

breakfast for themselves while their parents slept in or got ready for work. It also made it easy for kids to eat breakfast while watching TV.

At $1.29 each, Breakfast Mates cost about five times as much as the same cereal delivered in traditional packaging. If all US Americans ate breakfast this way for a year, it would generate 5.6 million tons of packaging waste.

Kellogg's pulled Breakfast Mates off the shelf a year after it was introduced. The problem with the product was not the idea of kids flying solo for breakfast. Nor was the problem all the artificial ingredients in the cereal and milk. After all, most fast-food restaurants sell strawberry-flavored milkshakes that contain no strawberries but instead feature more than forty factory-made chemicals, among them ethyl nitrate and amyl butyrate. The problem was that not even kids liked the idea of pouring warm milk over cereal, no matter how convenient it was and no matter how much TV the Breakfast Mates allowed them to watch.

The failure of Breakfast Mates notwithstanding,

there has been a severe social toll of all those mateless kids eating meals alone in front of the television, rather than sitting at table with family over a meal. When we divorce ourselves from the table, we lose a lot in the settlement; the food we settle for is not only less nutritious and more potentially harmful, it is also fundamentally less satisfying. The taste is flat, the temperature tepid, the whole experience lifeless. No wonder we redirect our attention from the food to the television. And yet so much of television is equally flavorless, harmful, lifeless. Some scholars have even named television watching *the* single most important factor in explaining the decline of civic life.[1] The television, as an isolating medium—rather than facing one another, we face the screen; rather than engaging whole people, we consume two-dimensional characters and personas—supplants the table and spawns a "moral minimalism" in which people, even from the same family, are indifferent to each other, cold, uncaring, and disconnected.[2]

---

*We're going to watch the end of the world
on television until the TVs go out.*

Derrick Jensen, "Beyond Hope"

THE PERILS OF EATING ALONE

Food is something good to eat. But it's so much more than that. Food is also something good to do, good to connect with, good to think over, good to play by, good to romance around. Even the Greek and Roman gods sat down for dinner together twice a day, even though they would live forever whether they ate or not. Eating together is social more than it is necessary.

Adam means "human." *Eve* means "life." A human needs another for "life" to come alive and become living. Identity can't grow ferally, only communally. We were meant to eat together, not solo. Eve's solitary eating is what got her in trouble.

At age sixteen Louis XIII (1601–1643) took power as king of France. Having exiled his mother and executed her partisans, he claimed only two close confidants: Cardinal Richelieu, who really ran the state, and the court jester Marais. Marais once kidded the king that "there are two things about your job I couldn't handle—eating alone and [excreting] in company."[3] The exaltation of a monarch was such that few were fit to dine with one. Meanwhile, as many as eight "grooms of the stool" waited on kings when at privy.[4] A king sat alone at the table and in company at the "throne."

If the primary biblical image of heaven is a banquet table and party, many artists' favorite image of hell (Bosch, Sartre, and others) is a table where we sit alone and serve ourselves. The famous picture of loneliness, Edward Hopper's lunch counter at a downtown diner ("Nighthawks," 1942), may even be surpassed in its hellish creepiness by the real-life photograph of John Paul Getty dining alone at the end of a long table at Sutton Place. Before you can find the lone diner in the photo (published in Clive Aslet's 2013 collection *An Exuberant Catalogue of Dreams*), your eye must hack its way through a dense, golden jungle of candelabras, epergnes, and tureens, all of which weigh down the table and hide the food.[5] The misery of riches may have never been better portrayed than in this photograph.

> *Hell is oneself.*
> *Hell is alone, the other figures in it*
> *Merely projections. There is nothing to escape from*
> *And nothing to escape to. One is always alone.*
>
> T. S. Eliot, The Cocktail Party (1949)

What makes human eating unique is that we eat together and talk about eating at a table with eating rituals that open our eyes to what we are eating. In German, there is a distinction between *fressen* ("guzzle") and *essen* ("dine"), between devouring food like an animal and savoring food like a human. God designed eating not just for survival but also for pleasure. A meal feeds the soul and spirit as much if not more than it feeds the body. That's why to "taste" in Greek also means to "enjoy."

Of course, any human relationship has the capacity

for hurt, and sometimes the pain of loneliness and isolation is less severe than the pain of contact and connection. But there is no better way to get out the kinks
in the human spirit, or heal the rifts in a family, or
unwind the twists in the order of the universe, than to
bring on the table.

In every home I've ever known
the living room's a tomb.
In every home I've ever known,
the dining room's the room.

Quoted in Adam Gopnick, The Table Comes First

THE END OF THE TABLE, THE END OF THE NEIGHBORHOOD

The two pillars of contemporary eating are the micro-
wave and the menu. Food is either something you
nuke or something you order; you get it by a drive-
through or by delivery.

These pillars are reflected in home construction.

Homes used to have two tables, a dining room table and a kitchen table. Then we did away with the dining room for the "great room," which consolidated the dining, family, and receiving areas of a home into what the *New York Times* called "the McMansion's signature space."[6] At the same time, the kitchen table gave way to the kitchen island, with stools all facing one direction, rather than chairs all facing each other.

As the table goes, so goes the neighborhood. Not too long ago, neighbors generally kept their doors open to one another. Smaller houses seemed less confining, because the more porous divisions between homes—separated not by doors of wood or steel but by "screen doors"—encouraged socializing with neighbors.[7] Neighbors would pop in and out, often unannounced, to borrow sugar or flour or just to chat, and the kids were easily monitored as they played outdoors in the yard or the street. An open door symbolized that in this neighborhood people mattered, relationships mattered. Even food mattered.

Munsey Park in Long Island, New York, is an upper-crust bedroom community. On its 320 acres live about three thousand people, as of 2014. Like many communities, they are governed by a homeowners association with gobs of rules, including permit requirements for all structural work done on homes, down to door or window replacements. You can't even put up a basketball hoop in your yard without board approval. In this quiet neighborhood riddled with Tudor homes and sycamore-lined streets, all street play is banned. No street soccer. No street basketball. No street baseball. No street scooters. No street Frisbee. No negotiation.

You may be reading this and thinking, *So, what's the problem?*

Street games are dying out, and with them an essential ingredient in community formation: the strong relational ties that are built when we let our guard down with each other, when we claim common space as an appropriate forum for play. In 2011 Texas mother Tammy Cooper spent the night in jail, charged with child endangerment. Her crime? She allowed her two kids, ages six and nine, to play on their scooters on their cul-de-sac as she supervised them.[8] Words like *stickball, skelly, stoop-ball,* and *street hockey,* and all they mean to the social and emotional development of children, will be lost to future generations if we don't break the suburban tyranny of the auto-cracy where car is king and screen is queen.

Chi beve solo si strozza.
The one who drinks alone, chokes.

Old Italian saying

IS THE TABLE ELITIST?

The biggest pushback I receive when I make the case to bring back the table is the accusation of classism. The Norman Rockwell picture of the family dinner table smacks for some people of elitism at best, racism at worst. I am reminded that families today are so diverse, so dysfunctional, so overburdened with duties and the day-to-day challenges of survival that for me or anyone to put this expectation on them is cruel and insensitive. "You, Sweet," they tell me, "of all people, as a futurist, you should know this already."

It is true that behind every "What's to eat?" is a host of purchasing, preparing, setting up, and cleaning up presuppositions. Most of us are clueless about how the food on our plate gets in front of us, or what it takes to make it so good. Serving three meals a day is like painting three pictures a day; the chef's palette is a combination of palate pleasures derived from earth, wind, fire, and water.

Every parent has to feed their kids somehow, some way. If you choose to feed them Big Macs while they watch TV or play games on their iPads, you have made a value statement: "Our family connection is less important than your personal entertainment," perhaps, or "I'm too busy to have to deal with you while we all eat." But the value statement isn't whether you are a single parent and have limited time to cook or you work late into the evening. The value statement isn't whether you have money to cook a homemade three-course dinner or whether you pick up take-home from McDonald's. The value statement is about the choice of spending time together, whenever you can find it, at least several times a week, around a table, where you can connect together, talk together, bond together, share food (even if a snack) together. The value statement is about choosing relationships over isolation, making time even when time is scarce. Steve Jobs, one of the greatest innovators in human history, limited his kids' use of technology in the home. The inventor of the iPad wouldn't let his kids have iPads at the table. Every evening, Steve sat down for dinner with his wife and three kids at a long table in the kitchen, where no devices were allowed. Table time was reserved for discussions of history, politics, books, and current events, both on the world stage and on the stage of their own lives. It's easy to say you're too busy to spend time with your kids, neighbors, friends, church. But the truth is, you have made a value statement about what is important to you and what priorities claim top shelf in your life.

In Goethe's *Faust*, the devil purchases Faust's soul not in exchange for fame and fortune; Faust wanted to do more good for the world than anyone, and he saw his soul as a fair exchange. The devil's one stipulation was key: "You will never stop and say to the passing moment, '*Verweile doch, du bist so schoen!*'" ["Wait, you are so beautiful"]. Faust can no longer savor the joy and beauty of each moment; he could now love everyone in general very much, but no one in particular. Faust became a do-gooder who couldn't savor the very goodness in life.

Faust had good motives for doing good, but in wanting to be God, he gave up his humanity. As we pursue good goals in life, we need to be diligent to protect those aspects of ourselves that make us human, as God created us. Our basic human relationships are key in protecting our humanity. So even if you can't eat together every night, you can make sure you do it a couple of times a week, and you can make those times special. And even when you can't have a whole family meal, you can teach your kids to shut off the TV, put down their devices, and face each other as they eat and talk together.

They say that God is everywhere,
and yet we always think of God as a recluse.

Emily Dickinson

TABLE MANNERS

Being together around a table doesn't mean we aren't still alone. Everyone reading this book can summon up an image of a couple in a restaurant, two bodies eating together at the same table but on different planets in mind and spirit. Everyone can also, however, call up a similar image in which two people never say a word to one another and yet clearly cherish the shared silence of each other's space. What makes the difference?

Authenticity. Truth. Every table must have it.

When you hear the word *truth*, what comes to mind? If the first thing that pops into your head is a statement, or you start mentally searching for a proposition or principle or philosophy, that's not Christianity, that's another religion. Christianity has a very different understanding of truth.

Aletheia is one of those Greek words every Christian should know. It means "truth," but as we outlined in chapter 1, every word is distilled from a backstory, which is derived from a root metaphor. So what is the backstory and root metaphor of *aletheia*?

Aletheia literally means "unhiding," the state of "not being hidden." The root metaphor of "truth," then, is coming out of hiding. To live the truth is to reveal one's presence and personage, to "unconceal" oneself.

The originating story of Christianity (and its antecedent, Judaism) has an *aletheia* moment. One day God gets ready to do God's favorite thing: walk and talk in the garden with Adam and Eve as they ask "How does our garden grow?" kinds of questions. But no one is around. "Adam, Eve, where are you?" God asks.

From the shadows comes a voice: "We're hiding."

Thus the first untruth, the first lie, is that our sin has made God our enemy.

"Adam, Eve, why are you hiding?"

"We're naked." This is the second untruth, the second lie: We are unsafe in our unguarded state. We're hiding from ourselves. We suffer from a broken relationship with ourselves.

"Adam, Eve, why did you eat that pomegranate?" (Whatever the fruit really was, it wasn't an apple.)[9]

"Eve, the woman you gave me, made me do it," Adam says. "The serpent made me do it," Eve says.

This is the third untruth, the third lie: We are better off alone. We're hiding from each other. We suffer from a broken relationship with one another.

"Adam, Eve," God says, "you break my heart. Life is truth or consequences. You've made your choice. Now here are the consequences: Out of the garden. Out of Eden."

This fourth untruth, partially exposed in Eve's relationship with the serpent, is that there is no place for us. We're hiding from the ground we came from and the garden God put us in. We're hiding from the garden planet called Earth that God gave us. We suffer from a broken relationship with creation.

The rest of the Bible is a story of hide and seek: As we hide from God, God seeks us out, to repair and redeem us in those four broken relationships, those four lies. God's mission in the world is to restore to relationship a hardheaded and rebellious people in spite of our attempts to fake a persona to get along with others or to mask our insecurities in drugs and deals, work and wardrobes.

For the past fifty years of "seeker-sensitive" church,

we may have had our categories wrong. The people in the pews, trying to find God, are not "seekers"; as the story of the Bible demonstrates, they, and we, are hiders. God is the seeker. The Bible is not about "God, where are you?" The Bible is God calling out, "Adam, Eve, and all my children, where are you?" God isn't hiding from us. We are hiding from God.

We don't have our faces turned toward God in hunting and hunger. We have our backs turned toward God, fleeing in revolt and rebellion. God doesn't turn his back on us; it's we who, for whatever reason, don't turn back to God. God does not go AWOL on us. We are the ones who go AWOL on God and others. God is hungry for us, as Francis Thompson's 1893 poem "The Hound of Heaven" suggests.

> *I fled Him, down the nights and down the days;*
> *I fled Him, down the arches of the years;*
> *I fled Him, down the labyrinthine ways*
> *Of my own mind; and in the mist of tears*
> *I hid from Him, and under running laughter.*
> *Up vistaed hopes I sped;*

And shot, precipitated,
Adown Titanic glooms of chasmèd fears,
From those strong Feet that followed,
followed after.

At the apex of this hide-and-seek story God sends us himself in Jesus and calls us to live *aletheia*. A phrase used of Jesus in multiple Gospels is "he showed himself." This is the language of intimacy; it's also the language of truth, of unconcealing. In the Emmaus story, the phrase is the same, although the words are different: At table with two disillusioned followers of the crucified Christ, Jesus "opened the Scriptures" (Luke 24:32) and "their eyes were opened" (v. 31). God had revealed God.

To be sure, sometimes God plays peek-a-boo with us, especially when we're exposed in our embarrassing filth and shame. Sometimes God is *deus absconditus*, "the hidden God," because he does not want to coerce our love and loyalty; he respects our choice to withdraw and cover ourselves. When Jesus said that the Holy Spirit would "guide you into all the truth" (John 16:13), he didn't suggest that we would be driven, forced, overpowered or even seduced into truth by God. In the words of Blaise Pascal, God gives us signs with "enough light for those who only desire to see, and enough obscurity for those who have a contrary disposition."[10]

On the cross, Jesus himself sang of a God who "has not hidden his face from him but has listened to his cry for help" (Psalm 22:24). On the cross, God turned toward us as far as God could turn. Now it's our turn to turn around (*metanoia*) and come out of hiding—not just to hang out with God like Adam and Eve in Eden, but to let it all hang out with the God who let it all hang out when he hung on the cross for us, naked, vulnerable, unconcealed.

———

He who cannot reveal himself cannot love, and he who cannot love is the most unhappy man of all.

Søren Kierkegaard

———

The greatest word spoken in the Torah is *hineni*, Hebrew for "here I am." The best-known use is when

God calls individuals (e.g., Abraham, Jacob, Moses), but even God precedes some actions with the declaration *hineni* (e.g., Isaiah 58:9; 65:1)—here I am, no more hiding, evading, running, or concealing.

In one memorable interaction, Moses sees a bush burn and hears God call, "Moses, Moses!" Moses responds, "*Hineni.*" Then the voice of God instructs Moses to go back to Egypt, a place he had fled only a short time ago, and free the people from enslavement. Moses musters all the courage he can, and says, "Yes, Lord" (Exodus 3). In this and other instances, *hineni* is the precursor to significant action on God's part, through his willing servants. *Hineni* is, in this respect, both an affect (self-expression indicating emotional readiness) and an effect—the acknowledgment of covenantal responsibility to live a life of truth. To live in truth is to stand before the great I AM in our nakedness and guilt, to reject the temptation to hide from God's glory. By laying bare and facing the worst of ourselves, we reveal the very best of ourselves. In other words, *aletheia* is *hineni.* Truth is "Here I am."

The transparency of truth—this is essential for a

table to be a table. A table requires that people unconceal themselves from one another, that for all their faults and failures and foibles and fixations, they still say to one another, "Here I am." When people tell the truth to each other, and when they hear the truth from each other, it is a sacred moment.

LEARNING AS SECOND NATURE

The table is where we set boundaries for ourselves. These boundaries both tribalize our identity and allow us to trailblaze new paths through life.

The table is where tribal values are haloed by habit. Character is formed so subtly that our actions seem to be thoughtless—almost second nature. But "second nature" is not "human nature"; our second nature is cultivated through table nurture. The table is where you *learn* your second nature.

A table is where you develop your "tastes," but tastes are similarly not inherent to who we are; they are negotiated between our uniqueness as individuals and our association with a particular culture. Taste is tribal, not general; timely, not timeless. Our tastes are trained, in the same way that our holiness is trained. You don't suddenly have good taste in some area of life any more than you are suddenly holy. Training in anything takes time. The old hymn encourages us to "Take Time to Be Holy" precisely because holiness takes time.

Pope Gregory I (540–604) would disagree with me. Around AD 600 he defined five aspects of gluttony, one of which included "seeking out delicacies" to gratify the "vile sense of taste." Similarly, Francis of Assisi (1182–1226) kept a pouch of ashes on his belt to sprinkle on his food in case it started tasting too good. After all, God wouldn't want you to enjoy your food. Others don't denounce taste as "vile," but they nevertheless consider the idea of taste invalid, not worth talking about. As the old Latin saying puts it, *de gustibus non disputandum est* ("There's no disputing taste").

There is no one "right way" to do the Christian life. Your music, your clothes, your food, your driving, your furniture, your library, your coffee—they're all a matter of "taste." I have a "taste" for Southern gospel music, while my brother John has a "taste" for opera and my brother Philip has a "taste" for German "oom-pah-pah" music. But those differences in taste don't divide us, and neither do we need to conceal our tastes from one another to remain in relationship. To acknowledge the different tastes of one another is meant to be not an end but a beginning to a conversation.

"Taste" is actually a big deal. It's a big deal to learn the difference between Green Day and Gershwin, Maroon 5 and Mozart, Switchfoot and Soundgarden. Our tastes are matters of both absolute necessity and utmost indifference. There is value in discussing, even disputing, taste: By disputation (an ordered and reasoned debate) the church throughout history has refined its theological palate, developing a gourmet appreciation for the gospel. In this way disputation is a factor in sanctification. But the development of our taste isn't just related to abstract concepts such as theology; according to Timothy Radcliffe, the monastic discipline of fasting, or voluntarily going without food for a time, was not so much about *not eating* as it was "opening one's eye to the food on one's plate." Fasting facilitates tastefulness—"being at ease in eating, eating what was put before you, eating together in gratitude, eating no more than your body needs."[11]

One of the secrets of life is to learn the discipline of historical context from which you can see how personal and provisional tastes are, to locate your second nature against a larger backdrop. Our tastes are cultivated, our second nature curated, by engaging life with verve and vitality, acknowledging the inherent value in perpetuating what's significant to us. Our tastes are not a teapot tempest; we live with passion and strive for excellence. We live not merely according to human nature but according to our second nature, when we give due credence to our tastes.

PROTOCOLS OF THE TABLE

All taste is acquired taste. The table is where we acquire our tastes; it's also where we fend for them. The most sophisticated foods—mousse, meringues, souffles, whipped cream—involve the infusion of hot air. The most sophisticated tables likewise have hot air rising from them, as our table talk lofts the social into the sacramental, charging the room with heat and light, energy and excitement.[12]

At the table locavores, who otherwise only eat food grown in their "foodshed," teach their children the difference between a "Marco Polo Exemption," in which they make exception for nonlocal spices and oils,[13] and the desire for a drive-thru Happy Meal, which (according to Alice Waters, a chef, locavore, and restaurateur) is a "kind of activity" inappropriate for "our kind . . . to get involved in."

The table is where we learn protocols of the table and houseways of the home, which become protocols of life. We teach our kids at table how to be "in" the world but not "of" the world. As Jesus told his disciples, there are activities and values that may be acceptable to others, but "not so with you" (Matthew 20:26). Or as John Wesley wrote to Francis Asbury in 1788, "Let [other groups of people] do what they please, but let the Methodists know their calling better."[14]

A protocol of the Sweet table is, "Eat nothing; taste everything." (Or in its more elongated form, "You don't have to eat anything, but you have to taste everything.")

Children like what they like, the rationale goes, but how will they know what they like and don't like if they don't give every food a try? For example, of all the foods the Israelites craved from Egypt—cucumbers, melons, leeks, onions, and especially garlic—I'd be happy leaving all but the cucumbers behind forever.

Another protocol of the Sweet table is grace. Life feeds on life; animals and plants gave their lives for our sustenance, which is why grace before meals is not an option. I shudder to think of the verdict of our descendants on the prime rib we eat today.[15]

Another protocol of the Sweet table is quality coffee. Our table tutors a taste in beans. Heretics who deny the health benefits of coffee are dealt with mercilessly. We celebrate the insight of James Bond, who much prefers coffee to tea, which in the novel *Goldfinger* he denounces as "mud" and "one of the main reasons for the downfall of the British Empire." Thank you, Ian Fleming.

We have yet another rule at the Sweet table: "No digital." It's not just that the device is turned facedown.

Whether books or cells or iPads or computers, the table does not make room for tablets.

We also refuse to rush a meal. That doesn't mean we count thirty-two mastications for every mouthful of food; neither do we require one another to use every one of our molars for crushing and chewing. Even the fanciest dinner parties in the Victorian era lasted only two hours. But at the table we slow everything down from the pace of the day to enable our souls to catch up with our bodies. We catch up with each other, converse about life, share stories, and laugh. Check it again: Solemn, sullen, somber, and grave are *not* fruits of the Spirit.

The true decorations of a home
are the guests that frequent it.
Ralph Waldo Emerson

Another protocol of the Sweet table, one that often helps extend the life of a meal, is story time. If the stories aren't readily forthcoming, we play a game: "Stump the Storytellers." Everything in the Sweet home has a story; you don't fill your home with stuff, but with stories. The game, then, is to find something in the house that the kids or guests don't yet associate with a story—an item of furniture, or something hanging on the wall, something displayed in a bookshelf or hidden in a cabinet or cupboard—and see if my wife and I can tell the story behind it. If the item has lost its story, it goes.

Beyond these various protocols, at the Sweet table we make a point of preserving dining rituals of the Victorian era, one of which is the tradition of two desserts. When you think of the Industrial Revolution, don't just think of the steam engine and telegraph. Think dessert. Jesus never ate dessert as we know it— maybe nuts, honey, and fruits like figs—but dessert itself is a modern invention. Nevertheless, it fits the character of the feasts that Jesus described and affirmed. It even offers narraphors for our formation: Chocolate is a symbol of how rottenness can be scrumptious. (Chocolate, like other, less dessert-friendly foods such as yogurt, sauerkraut, cheese, wine, and bread, is made through a process of fermentation, which is, in effect, a rotting process.) My perfectionist daughter used to make the most magical, melt-in-your-mouth miracle dessert: "Oreo balls." I have bribed, cajoled, threatened, and pouted, like Esau begging Jacob for a bowl of stew, but my daughter won't make them anymore, because they don't come out perfect. Nevertheless, dessert remains a priority: We are admittedly desultory about desserts when only the family is present, but when guests grace our table, two desserts are mandatory.

SETTING THE TABLE AT HOME

Home can have various connotations. Home to me may not be home to you. And some of us are homeless. What does it mean to set the table in our home? It means that wherever we are present with those close to us, whether our "home" is in the home of another, on a street corner, in a tiny apartment, or in a manor house, we set the table in our home when we invite Jesus into our personal space and share that space together with those we call family.

Restoring the table to your home not only strengthens the bonds of your relationship with God and your family members, but it will give you the security, emotional stability, and spiritual maturity to recognize God as the giver of every good gift. When you set the table in your home, you invite all those in your family to "taste and see that the LORD is good" (Psalm 34:8).

SETTING THE TABLE AT CHURCH

— ❧ —

Lord Jesus, I give you
my hands to do your work,
my feet to go your way,
my eyes to see as you do,
my tongue to speak your words,
my mind that you may think in me,
Above all I give you my heart
that you may love in me your Father
and all mankind,
I give you my whole self
that you may grow in me,
so that it is you, Lord Jesus,
who live and work and pray in me.

LANCELOT ANDREWES (1555–1626)

THE CHURCH IS DIVIDED into two groups: the walk people and the talk people. The walk people invest their energies in their hands, feet, and knees; they see the works of Jesus and the acts of the apostles, and they go and do likewise, and they have little patience for idle talk. Talk people, by contrast, revel in the teachings of Jesus and the theologizing of Paul; they love the life of the mind and fear the erosion of doctrine through unthinking deeds. They put their energies into ears, eyes, and tongues: seeing no evil, hearing no evil, and speaking no evil.

What brings all these body parts together? The table. The Communion table in the sanctuary, and the table of communion in the fellowship hall—both are Lord's Tables that can turn the tables on real human concerns, such as poverty, persecution, and addictions. One of the most important ministries in any church? Who is your Minister of Food?

At every meal Jesus ate—meals with outcasts, outliers, officials, friends, strangers—Jesus was both guest and host. He graciously accepted (and sometimes even cajoled) invitations to meals in unexpected places. But wherever and whenever Jesus ate, Jesus' presence turned every table into an altar. On whatever table Jesus ate there was always a mystery food: his own body and blood. Every table where Jesus ate was a potluck meal, with the greatest offering being his presence, the very revelation of God. When Jesus is at table, the best thing on the table is not something you can finger, fork, or stick. The best thing on the table is the presence of God. The presence of Jesus turns a simple meal into a sumptuous feast. The smell of Jesus is no longer in the air when the food of Jesus is no longer on the table.

In a crumb of bread the whole mystery is.

Patrick Kavanagh, "The Great Hunger"

For those who follow Jesus, a new tradition was launched in the Upper Room in Jerusalem with the Last Supper. The unleavened bread and the cup of wine offered to his closest disciples at the end of the Passover meal marked the end of one era and the beginning of a new one. The new Passover he presented was an invitation to a Lord's Table where Jesus would always be present, where the offering of food and drink in the name of Jesus would transform whatever the meal, whatever the time of year, into a banquet.

At the Last Supper Jesus added something to the Seder meal they had gathered to celebrate. The Passover celebration begins with three plates filled with bitter herbs (horseradish), eggs, matzoh, shank bone, haroseth (paste of nuts, fruits, and wine), and vinegar and salt water. After the three plates comes a full meal, followed by the *afikoman*, or dessert. But instead of the traditional *afikoman*, Jesus invented a new dessert for his disciples. The "added" elements were the broken bread (his broken body) and the poured-out cup (the blood of the Lamb slain from the foundation of the world).

LET US EAT

In every culture, the best theater of faith is the table. But this is especially true in Christianity. Jesus did some of his greatest theological teaching at the table. It is where he served his best food for life. Of twenty-three parables in Luke's Gospel, more than fifteen (or almost 70 percent) of them feature food.[1]

- At Levi's house, he put on the table his theology of mission (Luke 5:27-32).
- At Simon's house, he put on the table his theology of grace (7:36-50).
- At a meal with five thousand seekers, he put on the table his theology of evangelism (9:10-17).
- At a Bethany supper with Martha and Mary, he put on the table his theology of relationship (10:38-42).
- At a meal with Scribes and Pharisees, he put on the table his theology of holiness (11:37-54).
- At a meal with lawyers and religious leaders, he put on the table his theology of the kingdom (14:1-24).
- At his last supper, he put on the table his theology of discipleship. (22:21-23)
- At the Emmaus supper with Cleopas and Mary, he put on the table his theology of Scripture (24:13-35).
- At his last supper on earth, with his male and female disciples, he put on the table his theology of incarnation (24:36-44).

The table is what returns us to the focus of our faith: Jesus. Christian theology is the art of table talk. The summit of Christian theology is reached on the table.

In a famous essay, Johann Wolfgang von Goethe suggested that Leonardo da Vinci's composition *The Last Supper* was intended to convey Christ's words, "One of you shall betray me."[2] Not so. *The Last Supper* portrays Jesus saying, "Take, eat: this is my body." Not Christ foretelling his betrayal, but Christ instituting his Eucharist. The whole painting radiates from his quiet presence in the midst of some rather enlivened disciples.[3]

Just as God gave us bread to build the body and wine to gladden our hearts, John Calvin wrote, Jesus gave us the blood of Christ in sacrament to "exhilarate" our souls.[4] The language sounds shocking, and it should: No other religion talks about God like this—God present in bread becomes flesh, God present in wine becomes blood. Our salvation is not through rules, rites, rituals, or religious principles. Our salvation comes through a God who comes to eat with us at table and to feed us with his very presence.

Speaking of the Eucharist, Augustine ventriloquizes Christ: "You will not change me into you like the food of your flesh, but you will be changed into me."[5] We do not just look at sacred food to sacrifice it or worship it. We eat and drink the sacred food as we touch, taste, and smell it. But the food on which we feast is not food, but Christ himself.

Christ is the bread, awaiting hunger.

Augustine of Hippo

TABLE AS LITURGY, TABLE AS COMMUNITY

When Jesus said at the Last Supper, "Do this in memory of me," the *this* he meant was the table. Just as the slogan for Nike is "Just do it," as an encouragement to be active, the slogan for Christianity could be considered "Just table it"—whatever you come across in life, bring it to the table.

Much of the church's history of division is tied to our understanding of the Communion table. But most theologians ask too much of the table in terms of theology and too little of the table in terms of community. It is more important that our churches have tables that are relationally correct than liturgically correct. Rules aren't "truth"; we don't follow out of slavish obedience to something absolute. We follow preestablished rules because we want to signal our love of community and our respect for ancestral traditions (for example, Acts 16:3; 1 Corinthians 8:13). But rules should not get in the way of relationship. If I want to drink out of the same well as you, do I need to use the same cup, or can I use my own cup? Must the church insist on a one-size cup, or is it enough for Christ to be the living water that fills the well from which we all draw?

One of the greatest hymn writers in Christian history, Isaac Watts, put the theology of the table into musical form in his hymn "Jesus Invites His Saints":

Jesus invites His saints
To meet around His board;
Here pardoned rebels sit and hold
Communion with their Lord. . . .

We are but several parts
Of the same broken bread;
One body hath its several limbs,
But Jesus is the Head.

Let all our powers be joined
His glorious name to raise;
Pleasure and love fill every mind,
And every voice be praise.

The table is where a diverse body of Christ joins together. But in our fierce internal debates over table rules, we have let the table's central value slide. For some traditions, the table is a converting ordinance open to all; for other traditions, the table is an ordinance open only to the converted and baptized. Even the early Methodists restricted attendance at one of their "Three Meals of Methodism." While the family meal and the missional meal of Holy Communion were considered open to all, ironically the "love feast" was a closed table.[6]

Maybe we ought to exhibit more of the spirit of

John Calvin, who admitted that some things were beyond his pay grade. When it comes to the Lord's Supper, he said, "All that remains then is to break forth in admiration of the mystery which the mind is as inadequate to comprehend as the tongue is to express it."[7] Even the theologian whom some see as the greatest in church history, Thomas Aquinas, leaned toward an open table (even though he limited it to the baptized):

> If they be not open sinners, but occult, the
> Holy Communion should not be denied them
> if they ask for it. For since every Christian,
> from the fact that he is baptized, is admitted
> to the Lord's table, he may not be robbed of
> his right, except from some open cause.[8]

The church as the body of Christ is a communion of subjects—saints and sinners. Religion makes church into a collection of objects—rules, regulations, rituals, and resolutions. The subjects in the room are secondary; the regulations are the highest priority, the rules rule. A person subject to religion is deemed "in" or "out" based on her compliance to the almighty Rs. A growing church must consciously confront the "In-N-Out" issues that come with the "ownership" and "regulation" of the table. It is a fine line that separates valuing your "own" church and investing in God's mission there, and sensing you "own" the church and the church is "yours" because you donated money to "pay for it" and its ministries. An ownership church culture is more prone to wrap itself in red tape than to cut red ribbons.

When the church is no longer seen as an open place for the Spirit to play or the community "commons" where God makes miracles happen, the "In-N-Out" condition kicks in. We have trouble allowing "in" people who are not like us, and we hesitate to go "out" to be with people different from us. It's difficult for "In-N-Out" churches to "serve up something new"—to arrange their tables differently, to invite new people. An old Arabic greeting, "*Ahlan wa sahlan*," loosely translates as "May you arrive as part of the family, and tread an easy path as you enter." How many of our churches speak the opposite greeting when strangers enter: "You arrive as an outsider, and we'll make your path into our community as difficult as possible."

Our churches are not "ours." The Communion table doesn't "belong" to us. It's the Lord's Table; we all are merely guests. To be a good church means we allow Jesus to be the true Head of our Table. We accept our role as guests and not hosts, and we welcome whatever other guests our Lord invites to table with us.

Loaves of bread are the face of God.

Lazarillo de Tormes (1554)

BE THE BANQUET

One of my all-time favorite movies is *How to Train Your Dragon*. So when *How to Train Your Dragon 2* came out, I had to be one of the first to see it. So at its first 3-D showing, there I was, the first one in line to buy a ticket, the first one to enter the theater where it was showing.

Out of the five hundred available seats, I walked up the steps to the top tier of the theater and picked an end seat three rows from the back on the right—the most quiet and secluded of the bunch, I thought.

After I got settled in, a couple of Asian girls, teenagers, walked into the theater. They looked around, saw where I was sitting, and made a beeline in my direction, sitting directly in front of me. Next an Indian family walked into the theater—a mother, a father, a grandmother, and three children. They too looked around, saw where we were sitting, and took the seats directly behind me.

Now I started to feel crowded. Over the next twenty minutes, about another hundred people came to this showing, and—guess what?—with only a couple of exceptions, every party of every tribe, tongue, and nation, clustered in my little corner. The entire theater was a vast void of empty seats except for a crowded pocket of people huddled in the upper right corner of the cinema.

The human species is a lemming species. We are pack animals. We see what other people are doing, and then do the same thing. This explains why franchises are so successful. We complain about standing in long lines, but we actually pay big bucks for the privilege. Why are you paying five bucks for a Frappuccino? You're paying for the social interaction, the experience of ordering with others, the privilege of waiting with others for something that everyone deems desirable. The old-fashioned "bandwagon" continues today with daily tweets and retweets of what is trending. We happily go along for the ride, wherever the wave of public opinion is heading.

In a classic episode of *Candid Camera*, a man walks into a doctor's waiting room. All the other patients are in their underwear, their clothes all together in an orderly pile. The man briefly surveys the strange situation, then slowly removes his outer garments, neatly placing them next to the other patients' clothing, and then takes a seat. In another episode a man gets on an elevator and sees that all the other passengers are facing the back wall. He hesitates, but then does what all the others are doing: turns his back on the door and faces the back wall.

We easily become human pack animals. We live lemming lives. When Pilate asked the crowd which prisoner he should release—a convicted thief and lifelong scoundrel or a pious rabbi who legally had done no wrong—the crowd piled into the Sanhedrin's wagon and shouted, "Give us Barabbas!" (John 18:38-40). Jesus was crucified by a bandwagon.

And yet God made us in so many ways wholly and totally different from one another. As Jesus offers up to the Father his own personal "Lord's Prayer" (John 17), he closes by praying for "oneness" among all those who follow him as his disciples. Does this mean that Jesus wants us all to be the same—cloned Christians and cookie-cutter churches? Did Jesus inaugurate a franchise faith, a lemming life, a monotone mission?

Every great man is unique.

Ralph Waldo Emerson

In Redding, California, I was speaking at the church of one of my students. He bragged on an Italian restaurant, which a couple of foodies had been cultivating for the community for over a decade. The restaurant was only half full, but the food was delicious. That very day, the results were made public of the "Restaurant Favorites" of Redding, California. Guess the "favorite" Italian restaurant of Redding, California? "Olive Garden." In city after city, year after year, when the votes are counted and the majority has spoken, the "best" Italian restaurant turns out to be Olive Garden. So much for those hard-working chefs trying to preserve the tradition of authentic Italian cuisine.

The more you refine your tastes—the more gourmet your gospel—the less satisfied you will be with a franchise faith. Every church and every disciple of Jesus must decide: Do I want to be an Olive Garden, or do I want to be an Eden Garden? An Eden Garden is a garden of dreams, of imagination and beauty and hope. An Eden Garden church opens its doors to others in anticipation of what new life will enter.

In the words of poet Gerard Manley Hopkins, God made "all things counter, original, spare, strange."[9] It's not easy swimming upstream, against the current, remaining true to our "counter, original, spare, strange" design. But this is the narrow way that Jesus calls us to follow. Jesus didn't want us to be culturally captive. The bride of Christ is not a mistress of the moment or a pimp for the status quo. The bride of Christ is a pioneer of possibilities and harbinger of a new humanity. We are to live, Paul says, not according to human nature, but human nurture, when the nurturing of the human is done by the Spirit (Romans 8:4). Our true destiny is not human nature, but a new kind of human, a Jesus kind of human who is nurtured and nourished at the table.

You are to be taken, blest, broken and distributed, that the work of the Incarnation may go forward.

Augustine of Hippo

TABLE EVERYTHING

When you pray, "Thy kingdom come, Thy will be done," what difference will it make? How will you arrange your church accordingly?

Table it. Table everything. Whatever and whenever, bring it to the table.

Got doubts and disarray in your life? Table it. Daniel Boone was once asked if he had ever been lost in the woods. No, he replied, "but once I was perplexed for a few days." How many of us are "perplexed" about something—and for more than a few days? Paul once admitted to being "perplexed, but not driven to despair" (2 Corinthians 4:8, NRSV). The table that God set before Paul did not guard against perplexity, but it did guard against despair.

Got some conflicted relationships—people who have attacked you and hurt you, whose very presence causes gruff intestinal rumble? The table reduces fighting. It has been proven that one of the secrets to a successful marriage and loving family is to eat before you argue. Blood sugar levels correlate with irritability and annoyance;

low glucose levels escalate tensions and heighten tempers.[10] The same goes for the body of Christ. The secret of a loving, forgiving church is to commune before you argue. In feeding you, I forgive you.

Got some "parasites" you'd like to deal with? Table it. The word *parasite* comes from the Greek word for "hanger-on," someone who sticks around to get a free meal. An example of Christian parasites might be people who feed off of Christian images and stories while not really being part of the body. I had a conversation with a pastor who doesn't believe in the Trinity, doesn't believe in Jesus other than as a good teacher, doesn't believe that the Bible is in any way any more authoritative than Shakespeare, doesn't even like the traditions of the church. What she does like is the moral teaching, the "biblical values" and "Christian worldviews" that make up a tabletized religion. "So why call yourself a 'Christian,'" I asked, "if all you do is use Christianity as a rallying cry to be good?"

She responded, "You know, that's a good question."

So I tabled it. I ate with her, and as we ate I fed her the hot-cross sticky-bun called *Jesu Christos.*

How did Jesus win people over? Not by standing against them or arguing with them, but by walking alongside them and inviting them to the table.

———

I'm glad, I'm very glad
The Table of the Lord is spread
I'm glad, I'm very glad
The Lord has provided this bread.

Virginia Carle, sung to the tune of "Swing Low, Sweet Chariot"

———

Got a need for silence? Table it. Every exhalation is propelled by an inhalation. Outbursts of creativity require intakes of stillness and silence. Nothing comes forth without something doing nothing.

Why does it seem that the stronger the opinion and the louder it is expressed, the weaker the intelligence and experience backing up the opinion? Disciples of Jesus who return from the mission field are like soldiers who return from the battlefield. The experience makes them not louder but quieter; they don't pontificate, but stay humble, silent, considering when to leave things unsaid and when to simply listen to others.

Sometimes it is not speech but silence that testifies best to the truth. Sometimes it is not speech but silence that helps heal the pain. There is an old English saying, "Least said, soonest mended." This silence of the table is not a silencer-clean form of violence but the silence of truth. The greater the truth, the less that's said, the louder the silence, the more serene the spirit. The table is where the church can offer silence to a culture that fills every space with sound.

Got that feeling of being lost in the crowd, a loner who doesn't belong and doesn't fit in? Table it. Or maybe better in this case, "Pesto it." The most famous Latin phrase in US history, *E Pluribus Unum*, appears on the Great Seal of the United States. It was chosen by Benjamin Franklin, John Adams, and Thomas Jefferson, and most scholars assume they borrowed it from the masthead of the popular London periodical *The Gentleman's Magazine*. But Adam Gopnik, staff writer for *The New Yorker*, has made a compelling case that the real source for this motto was a recipe for an Italian salad, found in a poem attributed to Virgil (70–19 BC), called "*Moretum*" or "The Pesto."

> *It manus in gyrum; paullatim singula vires*
> *Deperdunt proprias;*
> *color est E pluribus unus.*

> *Spins round the stirring hand; lose by degrees*
> *Their separate powers the parts, and comes at last*
> *From many several colors one that governs.*[11]

The poem describes a farmer making an early form of pesto, a word that comes from the pestle and mortar used to make a salad by "pestling" together parsley, onions, cheese, garlic, and roux. The "pesto" would be seasoned with salt and coriander, and sprinkled with oil and vinegar. The secret of pesto is that each ingredient keeps its unique identity, but by being "pestled" together they form a new flavor. Out of many, one—and yet the many remain.

The life of maturity is the journey from the many to the one, without leaving the many behind.

Something new and unique emerges when the many come together to dance as one without compromising each other's manyness. It was at the table that Jesus made the shift from Judaism's particular covenant with a chosen people to a universal brotherhood reborn of the Spirit and naturalized as citizens of a New Jerusalem. The church has a seat at the table for everyone. There is no one who doesn't belong, no matter how different you are.

Got problems passing on your faith to your children? Table it. I am here today, writing a book about the table, because of four words spoken to me when I was thirteen years of age: "Your church needs you." The person who spoke those words was my pastor, Dr. Lawrence Snow (1900–1998). He was senior minister of a thousand-plus member United Methodist church, with a Bible-belt choir that filled four rows in the front, a balcony full of worshipers every Sunday, a junior and senior high youth group—each one with fifty-plus kids—and a four-keyboard Tracker pipe organ, strategically located in back of a central pulpit so that the two most prominent visuals were the front of the preacher and the back of the organist.

I was on my way out of the house one Friday evening to play basketball when the phone rang. "Lenny," my mother said, "the phone's for you. It's Dr. Snow." I stopped dead in my tracks. Dr. Snow had never called before, and I had only had quick exchanges with him in church. What could he want? My guilty conscience quickly went to the church steeple, and the daughter of the district superintendent, and . . . that's all I'm going to say.

With the trembling hands of anyone caught in their trespass and transgressions, and ready to confess, I picked up the phone and said feebly, "Hello."

"Lenny, this is your pastor. I'm calling you now because your church needs you."

"Sorry, sir. What did you say?"

"Lenny, your church needs you. That's why I'm calling."

With perceptible relief, I replied, "What can I do, Dr. Snow?"

"Miss Downs has eloped."

I waited for more, but that was all he said about the

church organist and choir director. So I replied, "Well, good for her. That's great."

"Yes, that may be good for her, Lenny, but it's not good for the church. We have no organist and choir director this Sunday."

"Oh, that's right," I said. "When is she coming back?" I asked.

"You don't understand. She's gone. Forever. She's not coming back. And that's why I'm calling you. I have found someone to direct the choir, but I need an organist."

I racked my brain thinking of someone to recommend, but came up empty. "I'm sorry, Dr. Snow, but I don't think I know of anyone to tell you."

"I'm not calling you for a name. I'm calling you because I want you to become the church organist."

"I'm sorry, Dr. Snow, but I've never played the organ in my life."

"Yes, I figured that, but you play the piano. And you'll learn."

Surely Dr. Snow would listen to reason. "But the piano only has one keyboard. The church organ has four."

"Forget three of them. Just play on one."

"But Dr. Snow, there are all those pedals on the floor."

"Just pretend they're not there."

"But Dr. Snow, there are all those stops that you have to pull in and out. I don't even know how to turn the organ on."

"I'll be at the church in an hour and I'll show you all you need to know to get started."

So at age thirteen I became the organist of a megachurch. I used my paper-route funds to take organ lessons, and playing the organ for churches, weddings, and funerals helped fund my collegiate and graduate education. Even after I deconverted from Christianity at age seventeen and spent the next six years in the liminal swamplands of atheism, Marxism, and other "isms" (which were really embolisms), what kept me tracking with the stream of Christianity? Despite my doubt and disbelief, every Sunday I was immersed in the truth of the gospel and the community of the table. Every Sunday I could not escape the claims of Christ in my life.

Irish novelist Bernard MacLaverty recalls a key detail of his Belfast childhood: "The air was full, always and everywhere, with the sound of the old ones talking."[12] Do the ears of your kids ring from the sound of the old ones talking? Ask those who have given their lives to children and youth, like Presbyterian pastor Lars Rood: "Kids gravitate to the oldest person in the room if that person shows an interest in them."[13] Children belong at the table. Teenagers belong at the table. They can be a pain, and they may ruffle the tidiness of the table. But if your eschatology is strong, if you have a vision of the future, they become a joy and a pleasure. The table talk they experience there gives them a sense of their place in the story, so that even if they leave the table, like I did, they can't escape it.

Got no church? Afraid to walk in that vast, huge stone building with the steeple and pillars? Alone without community? Table it. The church can set a table for anyone anywhere because the church is not a building, but a body—relationships around a table, headed up and hosted by Christ. Bishop Kenneth Delany, senior pastor at City Life Church in the Philadelphia area, reminds us that the first worshiping unit was not a large gathering in a large building but a family in a home. Every day the bishop conducts Communion—complete with a full meal—in his home for whomever shows up. He is bringing back the family altar, but is replacing the kneeler or *prie-dieu* with a full Communion table.

The ministry of food bridges the Communion table in our sanctuaries with the table of communion in the world. It is our unique offering to a world that has lost sight of the table as a source of quiet, of healing, of wholeness.

The legendary performer Frank Sinatra suffered through years of embarrassing failure in the early '50s. During that season of shame when his career was crashing, he often ate his lunch alone, shunned by the people he called "my fair-weather friends."

The one exception was Pasquale "Patsy" Scognamillo, the owner of Patsy's on West 56th Street, who would sit with Sinatra as he ate his lunch. One year, on the eve of Thanksgiving, Sinatra quietly made a reservation with Patsy to eat alone the next day, asking him to serve "anything but turkey." Sinatra didn't want to be alone on Thanksgiving, but he wanted to forget that he had nowhere to be. The restaurant was supposed to be closed on Thanksgiving, but Patsy didn't tell Sinatra that. Instead he invited the families of the restaurant's staff to come in for dinner, so the singer wouldn't be alone.

Many years later, Sinatra discovered Patsy's quiet act of generosity toward him—and that's why he never stopped coming to the restaurant, even when he worked his way back to the top of the entertainment world. Many wondered about Sinatra's perplexing loyalty to Patsy's over the years, but Pulitzer Prize–winning columnist Bob Greene says, "It was no big secret to the Scognamillo family. They all knew. A person recalls how he is treated not when he is on top of the world, undefeated, but when he is at his lowest, thinking he will never again see the sun." Patsy demonstrated grace to Frank Sinatra by opening his table to him; as stewards of the Lord's Table, we should certainly do no less. When we sit at the table together in our churches, what will be on your table?

SIX

SETTING THE TABLE IN THE WORLD

— ❧ —

Pleasing to the eye and good for food.

GENESIS 2:9

THE CHURCH USED TO throw the best parties. I mean, parties for the whole community, lasting not just for a couple of hours, but for days. Not anymore; we don't have time for parties. We have too many goals to tend to. One wonders whether our goal-seeking has replaced God-pleasing. The church may have learned to do pot-lucks. But can we do block parties? Can our vast parking lots become venues for tale-gating parties, where stories are shared and relationships are strengthened? It is not enough for the church to sponsor meals-on-wheels pro-grams; the church needs to become a meal-on-wheels.

We don't love our neighbors merely by not bothering them or by doing nothing bad to them. We love our neighbors when we reach out to them, when we listen to them, when we "give them something to eat" (Matthew 14:16). We love our neighbors when we share a table with them, when we bless and break bread together. Jesus likened the kingdom of heaven to going to a party where you don't have to prepare the food or clean up afterward. If that's how Jesus pictured the kingdom of heaven, shouldn't that be the image we show to the world? The firstfruits of the future, the earnest of eternity, the foretaste of what heaven is going to be like, is found where? For Jesus, at the table.

I used to think hospitality was a lost art. Now I'm convinced it is a lost *heart*. There is a Sankrit saying, *Atithi Devo Bhavah*, which translates, "The guest is God" or "guest becomes God." How we treat a guest, according to this saying, is literally how we are treating God. Of course there's a long, biblical foundation for this idea, but it gets particularly interesting when you consider that the word "hospitality" derives from *hospes* ("guest, host, stranger"), which itself derives from *hostis* ("stranger, enemy"—our English word "hostile" comes from *hostis*).

The English word *rival* has a similar backstory and a root metaphor. *Rivales* in Latin meant not "opponents" or "competitors" but neighboring communities on the two opposite banks of a common stream. Even as recently as Shakespeare's era, *rival* meant "companion." People who live on two sides of a stream (or lake or ocean) should be rivals in this classic sense, but often they are rivals in the more contemporary, more tragic sense.[1] To restore rivals as companions, we need to get both parties to the table.

Have your breakfasts all alone.
Share lunch with your best friends.
Invite your enemy to dinner.

Nelson Mandela

During the days when Anabaptist (Free Church) groups were being persecuted throughout Europe, an old Mennonite minister in Emmenthal, in the canton of Bern, in the heart of Switzerland, practiced the literal meaning of hospitality. Early one morning, he heard men on the roof of his house, tearing off the tiles and throwing them to the ground in an attempt to drive him out of town. Arising from bed, he asked his wife to prepare a good breakfast for the men. Then he went outside and invited them to breakfast, insisting that they come in and eat since they had been working so hard. Shamefacedly they came in and sat at the table. He prayed for them and their families, then served them breakfast. After they had eaten they went out and put the tiles back on the roof.[2]

More recently, Magic Johnson and Larry Bird faced each other on the basketball court as arch-competitors—first in high school, continuing through college, and culminating in the NBA, with Johnson playing for the LA Lakers and Bird playing for the Boston Celtics. The rivalry of these two champions became legendary—as did their dislike for one another, which seemed to grow in intensity with every passing year.

Somewhere along the way Converse paid each of

them to shoot a shoe commercial; they faced each other on the court, Bird wearing white shoes, Johnson wearing black. Bird insisted that they film the commercial at his farm in Indiana. The shoot began icily, with both superstars circling each other, but when they broke for lunch and started to go their separate ways, Bird's mother announced that she had made lunch and invited everyone to the table.

In Larry Bird's words, "It was at the table that I discovered Earvin Johnson. I never liked Magic Johnson very much. But Earvin I like, a lot. And Earvin didn't come out until I met him at Mom's table."[3]

That's the power of the table: We lower our guard as we break bread together; we become ourselves, and we become open to one another. We cease being rivals, enemies; and we begin to experience companionship, friendship.

A TABLE OF EQUALS

In the context of ancient hospitality, to "break bread" had specific meaning. Bread was divided according to status. Workers got the burnt bottom of the loaf ("the heel"); the family got the middle; and guests got the top, or the "upper crust."

In contrast to this hierarchy of hospitality, Jesus never took the biggest pomegranate or the largest chunk of honey. He always thought of others first and made sure there was an abundance of leftovers. In fact, whatever Jesus touched issued forth in superabundance.

The gospel is God's hospitality; God invites strangers to enjoy a meal and treats us as honored guests and family members. We are guests at God's table, just as the world we seek to reach are God's guests. Our focus on convincing and "evangelizing" along the lines of propositions, teaching didactically rather than through relationship and love and hospitality, shows how much we have systematized what is to be relationally mediated.

What does it mean for us to be a good table host, especially when we share table with people outside the faith? Moreover, how can we be a good guest when we are invited into the company of those outside the faith?

First, we must remember that the host can do no wrong. Alice B. Toklas, host of the most famous French salon in the world, used to say that "there is insofar as there is a hostess no failure."[4] When we remember that there is a host attending to us, we can be confident that nothing can go wrong. Every detail is covered.

One of the most primal of all taboos is public ingratitude to a host who shared their table with you.[5] Therefore, when we are guests, whether guests of God or guests of the world (or, in some cases, both), we should commit ourselves to being happy and grateful. Frankly, I have had some guests who look as if they'd be happier holidaying in the Gaza Strip.

Beyond basic gratitude, as guests we should treat our host's space as if it were our own home, not our outhouse. We also need to consider when we have outlived the graciousness of our host. There is a saying that the three most beautiful lights in the world are sunlight, moonlight, and taillights. A guest in the Middle Ages who had overstayed their welcome would be served a cold shoulder of beef. (Hence giving someone the "cold shoulder.") In colonial periods, house visitors stayed in a guest room with a four-poster bed. Pineapples were attached to the posts. When it was time to leave, a pineapple was removed from one of the posts. If you didn't leave, a second pineapple was removed; that meant you should leave within three days. If those three days passed, and you still hadn't departed, a third pineapple was removed. That meant you had twenty-four hours to get out or you'd be physically removed.

———————

Eating is more than an individual, biological act. Human beings are made to eat together, sharing their table with family and friends.

Jose A. Pagola, The Way Opened Up by Jesus

———————

ALWAYS BRING SOMETHING TO THE TABLE

A gift for the host(s) is always appropriate. It can be canned pears, or peach jam, or a bottle of wine. Or it can be something more creative. One of the greatest hostesses of eighteenth-century Paris, Sophie de Condorcet, included in her set of rules for a successful evening event a requirement for guests to bring something. But what they were expected to arrive with was a list of conversation starters. The expectation was that they would explore them "with the same rigor as a scholar in a library, except that rather than consulting books, the other guests were to provide the insights. Examples of fitting topics included: What is the wisest way to approach one's own death? Can governments make us good or only obedient?"[6]

Finally, a good guest will always leave something on the table. A Canadian friend and author, Margaret Terry, has recently become an empty nester. When I asked her one day how she has learned to cook for one after having raised a family, she replied:

> I haven't. I still cook for a family. I make chili
> for twelve and enough lentil soup to feed a
> kindergarten class. I share it with my dad, my
> sister's family, visiting sons and anyone in my
> community who's sick, troubled or who could
> use a bowl of comfort. Because that's what
> food is for me and that's what it gives me to
> make it. Comfort. Sharing it is the joy and
> the blessing.

A gift from a guest can have prophetic significance. If my two brothers and I heard this story once from my mother, we heard it a hundred times: A poor family with five young boys liked to host new people to their church for a meal in their home. During one such meal, a guest noticed that the youngest and smallest of the five boys was always the last one to get served. He was the last one to get his drink. He was the last to get passed the plates of food; in many cases the plates were almost empty by the time they reached him. His was the last piece of pie for dessert, and it was the smallest piece of all.

That guest was invited back to the family's home for dinner, and he volunteered to bring the dessert. After the meal was finished, he opened his bag and placed seven apples in a bowl. They all were of varying sizes, but six were big and beautiful, while one was small and wrinkled. Sure enough, the youngest ended up with that one. But when he bit into it, it didn't squirt apple juice. His teeth clanked on something solid. Hidden in the apple was a twenty-gram gold bar. Thanks to that story, two of us brothers always competed not for the biggest and best of whatever we were presented with, but for the smallest and most wrinkly.

———————

If you are not a missionary you need one.

Harold Bosley

———————

COMING AND GOING

As Christians, we are both minister and missionary. We have a ministry to the body, and a mission in the world. The critical word for ministry is "Come." We help people come to Christ. The critical word for mission is "Go." We go for and in Christ. But the referent of both "Come" and "Go" is Christ. Christ is both our departure and our destination.

Both our ministry and our mission take place in the world, which begins with our zip code. Jesus loved a postal code; he cried over a city he loved named Jerusalem. But he had a vision beyond Jerusalem and set tables in particular places, sometimes even controversial places, whether Nazareth or Galilee or Samaria.

Most churches are setting general tables rather than particular tables. I'd actually love to live generally rather than particularly, chasing summer campfires and forsaking winter committees. I'd rather live extensively rather than intensively, enjoying a perpetual cruise where all my needs are provided for, rather than dwelling where the sheets have to be washed, and the carpets vacuumed, and the meals prepped. I'd rather move away and escape than move in and engage. I'd rather not have to deal with the stark terrors and hard realities of the particular world in which we live.

Do what's in front of you.
Mother Teresa

But Jesus wants us to set a particular table, to demonstrate concrete love, not love in the abstract. My Gramma May's path to holiness was lined with baked beans. She lived with my aunt Charlotte and her family, and whenever someone Gramma May knew was sick, or seemed depressed, or had lost a loved one, she would tell one of my cousins, "Go tell _____ we are praying for her recovery," and she would send them off with a pan of freshly baked beans, wrapped up like a present, so thick they cut like a piece of cake. Every year, my birthday present was a pan of baked beans. (I added the vinegar.)

Our concrete expressions of table love can be quite provocative. A law was passed in a rough part of urban Philadelphia, making it illegal to give food to people in the street. Urban monk Shane Claiborne and his friends and fellow members of the Simple Way community had claimed that zip code in the name of Jesus, so they set up a table on the street and distributed "the Eucharist." Of course, in the high Eucharistic tradition of the church, once the bread and wine have been blessed, it is no longer food. So the cops watched as people were fed at the Lord's Table, and instead of arresting the People of the Simple Way, they took their hats off and reverently worshiped.

The power of the church setting a table in the world is showcased by the civil rights movement, where churches and church people took not just to the streets but to the lunch counters of the South. Lunch counters originated during the French Revolution; doctors and day-laborers could rub elbows there, share domestic gossip, and build democratic community.[7] In the South, however, lunch counters had become showcases of segregation. The symbolic significance of students integrating lunch counters in downtown department stores, in defiance of unjust laws, cannot be overemphasized. To protect the integrity of their effort, they followed a particular table etiquette while people threw salt in their eyes, dumped mustard on their heads, and stubbed lit cigarettes on their forearms.

- Do show yourself friendly on the counter at all times. So sit straight and always face the counter.
- Don't strike back, or curse back if attacked.
- Don't laugh out.
- Don't hold conversations.
- Don't block entrances.

The contrast between the civility of the protestors and the barbarism of the protectors of the status quo was stark and undeniable, and the lunch counter sit-ins were an early success story in the movement to confront the segregated South.

Our ancestors were, in many ways, more creative in setting a table in the world than we are today. One long tradition that spread through various cultures was drinking from a common cup called pass cups (German and Dutch), Quaich (Scottish), Tyg (English), or leather "love cups" (Viking). One of my special treasures is a walnut round container called a Grolla. Also known as a Friendship Cup, it's made of turned wood finely carved with six spouts and a cover. Handmade by only a few remaining workshops in the Valle d'Aosta in the Italian Alps, the Grolla ritual is built around the legend of the Holy Grail. From the Grolla you drink Café Valdostana, a blend of espresso and grappa, supplemented with Grand Marnier, Génépy, sugar and spices, or orange or lemon peel. The liquid in the Grolla is set on fire and then extinguished by a small round lid that sits on top. Persons who drink from the same Grolla commit to be united in friendship. While it is being passed, they toast each other, tell stories, and share dreams about the future. There is only one rule: The Grolla must be passed around, with everyone drinking from their own spout, but it can never be set down as long as there is liquid left in it. The Grolla is an "all in" friendship ritual, and the more turns around the table, the more the atmosphere warms up, the more the conversation flows, and the deeper the friendships get.

To deny the table is to deny fellowship, friendship, and "family." One of the best known but least understood stories Jesus told is the only story where he gave a character a name. That alone should catch our attention, like a Roman candle being lit over the text. But when the name Jesus chose for the character is also the name of his best friend, the story lights up like a Fourth of July fireworks display, demanding our careful attention. Sadly, neither of these semiotic flares is typically mentioned, much less probed, by biblical scholars; thanks to the versitis that plagues a tabletized faith, we are far more prone to take apart words than to connect narrative dots and unpack metaphors.

But God's breath is as much on the narratives and metaphors of Scripture as it is on the words. So we must look past the tamed and domesticated interpretations of the story of the Rich Man and Lazarus (Luke 16:19-31), which assure us that the rich man went to hell because he ignored the needs of the hungry. Charles Dickens found this story so predictable as it is traditionally interpreted that he wrote a new ending for it, which became *The Christmas Story* of Ebenezer Scrooge that we tell one another every year.

So much for Jesus upending the expected and startling us with the strange. But if we read this text as if the images and symbols mattered as much as the words, we quickly notice a few things. First, the rich man is "dressed in purple and fine linen" and ate sumptuously from the table every day (v. 19). In other words, this is a story about the Bill Gates of Jesus' day. This enormously wealthy individual allowed Lazarus, a homeless person with an advanced case of leprosy ("the dogs came and licked his sores," v. 21), to live at his highly secured front gate, where undoubtedly the movers and shakers of their society made daily passage.

Lazarus was fed the wealthy man's leftovers; does anyone *not* want leftovers from Bill Gates's table? Here is a magnanimous and charitable person of wealth who was doing more to take care of the poor and be on the side of the hurting than most of us reading these words: How many of you have homeless people living on your front porch?

So what landed this rich man in hell? The secret to unlocking the meaning of the story is hidden in two details.

One is the poor man's name of Lazarus, namesake of Jesus' best friend whose home was his favorite place on earth. The story alludes to hospitality and relationship from the outset.

The second detail is the arrestingly gratuitous data that the rich man had "five brothers." Again relationships are a key theme here, and the concern of the rich man for his brothers comes through clearly.

The rich man is in hell not because he didn't take care of the poor. He actually *did* take care of the poor. The rich man is in hell because he thought he had five brothers, when God actually gave him six.

While he helped Lazarus, he failed to form a lasting relationship with Lazarus. He failed to see Lazarus on equal footing with himself. He failed to love the person he was "taking care of." He failed to treat Lazarus as a person with head-to-toe human needs and aspirations.

This failure toward Lazarus was probably the rich man's failing toward others as well. As charitable as he was, he was self-centered rather than other-centered. He cared about poverty in general, but he wouldn't get his hands dirty with this particular poor man, Lazarus, who was right outside his door. He was in hell because, even though he fed Lazarus the charity case, he refused to invite Lazarus the person to table with him.

Jesus expects his followers to do more than ladle out food to the poor. Jesus expects his followers to treat the poor as our brothers and best friends, and ladle out love to them as we do our friends and relatives, around the table God has provided us.

I was once asked to travel from Seattle to London for a day of "strategic futuring" with all the heads of the Salvation Army from around the world. I agreed on one condition: that I could spend some personal time with General Linda Bond, the nineteenth general of the Salvation Army, the third woman ever to lead the organization.

General Bond graciously agreed to my request, and after a long day of strategic scenarios and trends analysis, we sat down for dinner together. Each of us ordered steak; hers was bigger than mine.

The Salvation Army by-laws make the person holding the top office of the charity the fiduciary owner of all Salvation Army properties worldwide. In other words, even though she was paid a meager salary, I may have been having supper with the wealthiest woman in the world.

"Do you have any idea why I asked for this time, General?"

"No, I don't. But I'm glad to share this meal with you."

"I only have one question. It's about Joan Kroc, the widow of Ray Kroc, and her gift to the Army. Why did 'St. Joan of the Arches,' as I hear she was called, a liberal Democrat, give the Army over two billion dollars—the largest gift in the history of philanthropy? How did you broker that gift?"

"Oh, she didn't give the money to me," the general replied. "She gave the money to the Salvation Army. And it wasn't 2.2 billion. The check was for 1.6 billion, although with compound interest and all that, it did get a whole lot bigger."

"I know, I know," I continued. "But I also know that no one gives big bucks, especially over 90 percent of their estate, to an institution. They give to a person who represents that institution. Why did Joan Kroc trust Linda Bond enough to hand her a check for 1.6 billion dollars? What was it that cemented your relationship?"

"Well, we did bond"—the general smiled at the inadvertent pun—"when she found out I was the thirteenth child of a coal miner. My father was a coal miner in Nova Scotia; my mother was an illegitimate child of a maid and a British lord. She was adopted and taken to Canada at age seventeen, and I was the youngest of their thirteen children."

"Why did your being the thirteenth child of a coal

miner's daughter make a difference to Joan Kroc?" I asked. "Rich girls don't marry poor boys, and vice versa?"

"Oh, no," General Bond replied. "Joan was an exception to that rule. She had 'humble beginnings,' as she called it. She was brought up very poor in a bad section of St. Paul. During the Depression, her father was mostly unemployed, and he often left the family without food or money or his presence. Her mother did the best she could teaching music lessons, and always made sure Joan had money for music lessons. But many times they were without food and without heat, and didn't know how they would make it through the week.

"The one thing Joan looked forward to as a child, that she knew was their salvation, was when a Salvation Army officer would come on Friday evening to deliver some bags of groceries. His arrival was the highlight of their week, she told me, because that meant she and her mother could be sure of food that coming week and not have to worry."

"I thought you had to go to the Salvation Army to get food," I said. "Wasn't that a bit unusual to have the food delivered to your home?"

"Yes. But the Salvation Army officer didn't just deliver food. He also sometimes came in, put the food on the table, and played with Joan—sometimes on the floor, sometimes on the table. He was a positive male figure for her as a child."

"In a sense, then, the person really responsible for this 1.6-billion-dollar gift is not Linda Bond but this Salvation Army officer."

"Yes," she said smiling with her characteristic humility. "You're exactly right."

"Do you know his name?"

"No. I don't think anyone does."

"Do you think he's still alive?"

"Almost positive he's not."

"So he died without knowing? He never knew the impact of his going the second mile, bringing some groceries to a home that might not have been able to get food any other way, and taking the time to play with a little girl whose father was often missing in her life."

"Yes, you could say that."

Here was a Salvation Army officer who, when he died, thought, *Well, I served for decades without anything really special happening. Just an ordinary ministry doing ordinary Salvation Army things. Nothing unusual or spectacular on my watch.* There's a lesson in that for us. The greatest blessing you will ever bestow in your life you may never know. And you don't need to know. We don't have to do spectacular things. We just have to keep doing what God has called us to do. In a very real sense, that boils down to bringing people to the table, and trusting God to take what we've planted and sown to bring in a harvest decades or generations later.

CONCLUSION

— ⚘ —

HENRY JAMES ONCE wrote that "summer afternoon" are the most beautiful words in the world. My pick? "Table's ready," followed by "What's to eat?"

Remember God's first command in the Bible? Eat.

Remember God's last command in the Bible? Drink.

And everything in between is a table—a life-course meal on which is served the very bread of life and cup of salvation.

It's time to bring back the table to our homes, to our churches, and to our neighborhoods and world.

You don't grow as a disciple of Jesus by sitting in a

church building soaking up the ink of a tablet, with its static statutes and impersonal instructions. You grow as a disciple by eating at a table. Some of the last words of Jesus in the Bible are found in Revelation: "Here I am! I stand at the door and knock. If anyone hears my voice and opens the door, I will come in and eat with that person, and they with me" (Revelation 3:20). There Jesus goes again: always wanting to eat at table with us. In fact, it is the Bible's favorite image of heaven— a place where, in the words of Robert Stamps, "God and Man at Table Are Sat Down."

> *Who is this who spreads the victory feast?*
> *Who is this who makes our warring cease?*
> *Jesus, risen savior, prince of peace,*
> *God and man at table are sat down*

Every Mother's Day, I go to YouTube and listen to Johnny Cash's version of the Ira Stanphill song "Supper Time."[1] The song reminds me of my childhood, when my mother would come to the door and call us home with the words, "It's supper time!" The last stanza of the song portrays heaven as Jesus did: a banquet table with plenty of food and plenty of room. Just as my mother used to call us home, so Jesus will one day call out those same words to us:

Come home, come home, it's supper time.
The shadows lengthen fast.
Come home, come home, it's supper time.
We're going home at last.

The meal is the message. The gospel is an invitation to go to Jesus' house for a meal. The life we live is the journey to that banquet, and we get there not by way of a tablet but by way of a moveable feast. Jesus is not a one-and-done meal-ticket. He is our manna; he is our mañana.

The Jesus command is not "Do it." The Jesus command is "Do this." When Jesus says to us at the table, "Do this to remember me," the "this" is the table. In other words, we are instructed to do "table" time in memory of Jesus. Whenever we break bread or sup or dine together, we are to re-member Jesus at our table.

Disciples of Christ: do table!

NOTES

INTRODUCTION: BRING BACK THE TABLE

1. Biblical scholar Robert J. Karris was the first to point to the connection between Jesus' eating habits and his subsequent sentencing and crucifixion. See Robert J. Karris, *Eating Your Way through Luke's Gospel* (St. Joseph, MN: Liturgical Press, 2006), 97.
2. Michael Pollan, *Cooked* (New York: Penguin, 2013).
3. Cody C. Delistraty, "The Importance of Eating Together," *Atlantic Monthly*, July 18, 2014, http://theatlantic.com/health/archive/2014/07/the-importance-of-eating-together/374256.
4. "The Family Dinner Challenge," *The Six O'Clock Scramble*, http://www.thescramble.com/family-dinner-challenge/.
5. "Television Statistics and Sources," Catholic Education Resource Center, http://www.catholiceducation.org/articles/parenting/pa0025.html.
6. Delistraty, "Importance of Eating Together."
7. National Center on Addiction and Substance Abuse, "The Importance of Family Dinners VIII," September 2012, http://www.casacolumbia.org/addiction-research/reports/importance-of-family-dinners-2012.
8. Dinner Trade, "Interesting Statistics on Family Dinners," http://dinnertrade.com/568/interesting-statistics-on-family-dinners.
9. Frøydis N. Vik et al., "Associations between Eating Meals, Watching TV While Eating Meals and Weight Status among Children, Ages 10–12 Years in Eight European Countries," *International Journal of Behavioral Nutrition and Physical Activity* 10 (May 2013): http://www.ijbnpa.org/content/10/1/58.

10. University of Minnesota, "Regular Family Meals Promote Healthy Eating Habits," *Science Daily,* November 18, 2004, http://www .sciencedaily.com/releases/2004/11/041116232104.htm.

11. Marla Eisenberg et al., "Correlations Between Family Meals and Psychosocial Well-Being Among Adolescents," *JAMA Pediatrics,* August 2004, http://archpedi.jamanetwork.com /article.aspx?articleid=485781.

12. "The Family Dinner Challenge," *The Six O'Clock Scramble.*

13. This is the argument of Alice Julier, *Eating Together: Food, Friendship, and Inequality* (Champaign, IL: University of Illinois Press, 2013).

14. Amanda Marcotte, "Let's Stop Idealizing the Home-Cooked Family Dinner," *Slate,* accessed September 10, 2014, at http://www.slate.com /blogs/xx_factor/2014/09/03/home_cooked_family_dinners_a _major_burden_for_working_mothers.html.

CHAPTER 1: EVERY STORY I KNOW BEST I LEARNED FROM A FLANNELGRAPH

1. I coined the term *versitis* in my book *Viral: How Social Networking Is Poised to Ignite Revival* (Colorado Springs: Waterbrook, 2012). See also my *Giving Blood: A Fresh Paradigm for Preaching* (Grand Rapids, MI: Zondervan, 2014).

2. See Sweet, *Giving Blood.*

3. See my book *The Greatest Story Never Told* (Nashville: Abingdon, 2012).

4. Nicodemus eventually got it, even helping to answer Jesus' prayer from the cross, saving his body from the encircling dogs and preparing his corpse for burial (John 19:39-42). Jesus sang from the cross, "Dogs are circling me. . . . Save me from the power of the dogs" (Psalm 22:16, 20).

5. *Fast Company,* October 2012, 18.

6. For this critique see Raymond Tallis, *The Kingdom of Infinite Space: A Fantastical Journey around Your Head* (London: Atlantic Books, 2008).

7. I am thinking here of such things as psycho-neurolinguistics and such scholars as George Lakoff, Eleanor Rosch, Mark Johnson, and Iain McEwan.

8. G. J. Stephens, L. J. Silbert, and U. Hasson, "Speaker-Listener Neural Coupling Underlies Successful Communication," *Proceedings of the National Academy of Sciences* 32 (August 10, 2010): 14425–30.

9. John MacArthur brings back this old preacher's story in *Our Sufficiency in Christ* (Wheaton, IL: Crossway, 1998), 241–42.

CHAPTER 2: "THOU PREPAREST A TABLE BEFORE ME"

1. For an extended discussion of this, see my book *Carpe Manana* (Grand Rapids, MI: Zondervan, 2001).

2. See the review of two books on Versailles by John Rogister, "All the King's Horses and All the King's Men," *Times Literary Supplement*, March 22, 2013, 13.

3. Andrew Root, "Who Am I? (Version 2.0): Adolescent Identity in a Digital Age," *YouthWorker Journal*, January/February 2010, 36–38.

4. For a discussion of ethics related to BIID, see Jonathan Wolff, *Ethics and Public Policy: A Philosophical Inquiry* (New York: Routledge, 2011), chap. 7.

5. For more on identity formation see my book *Me and We: God's New Social Gospel* (Nashville: Abingdon, 2014).

6. Lutherans and Baptists score the highest, in the mid-50th percentile. Pew Research Religion and Public Life Project, "Religious Landscape Survey," http://religions.pewforum.org/reports.

7. Brett Kunkle, "How Many Youth Are Leaving the Church?" *Truth Never Gets Old*, February 24, 2009, http://www.conversantlife.com /theology/how-many-youth-are-leaving-the-church.

8. For some preliminary probings of this identity issue in relationship to Jews and the Amish, see my book *The Well-Played Life* (Wheaton, IL: Tyndale Momentum, 2014), 98–104.

9. Closing comments from *The Amish Shunned: American Experience*, PBS, aired February 4, 2014.

10. For more on the Amish table, see my book *The Well-Played Life*.

11. See Jon Nielson, "3 Common Traits of Youth Who Don't Leave the Church," ChurchLeaders.com, http://www.churchleaders.com/youth

/youth-leaders-articles/159175-3-common-traits-of-youth-who-don-t-leave-the-church.html.

12. By calling the steeple a "pillar of remembrance," the museum engages in connecting itself to its story; such pillars were erected to mark significant moments in the Jewish experience. See, for example, Genesis 28:18; Exodus 24:4.

13. George Myerson, *A Private History of Happiness* (Katonah, NY: Bluebridge, 2012).

CHAPTER 3: JESUS, THE MESSIAH OF THE OPEN TABLE

1. Adam Gopnik, *The Table Comes First* (New York: Vintage, 2012), 309.

2. See Martin Luther's *Table Talk* to witness this principle being put into practice.

3. Gopnik, *The Table Comes First,* 41. Also featured at such meals was the "vomitorium," a contrivance that allowed guests to keep the party going.

4. Jodi Magness, *Stone and Dung, Oil and Spit: Jewish Daily Life in the Time of Jesus* (Grand Rapids, MI: Eerdmans, 2011), 81.

5. See, for example, Matthew 9:9-13; Mark 2:15-17; Luke 5:27-32.

6. Magness, *Stone and Dung, Oil and Spit*, 83. See Mark 14:20.

7. See the superb book on this by Frank Viola, *God's Favorite Place on Earth* (Colorado Springs: David C. Cook, 2013).

8. Conrad Gempf, *Mealtime Habits of the Messiah* (Grand Rapids, MI: Zondervan, 2005), 74.

9. Read Luke 24:29-30 in that light.

CHAPTER 4: SETTING THE TABLE AT HOME

1. Paul Ginsborg, *The Politics of Everyday Life* (New Haven, CN: Yale University Press, 2005), 111. See Robert Putnam, *Bowling Alone: The Collapse and Revival of American Community* (New York: Simon & Schuster, 2000), 231.

2. This is anthropologist M. P. Baumgartner's phrase. See his *The Moral Order of a Suburb* (New York: Oxford University Press, 1988), 3, 134.

3. Beatrice K. Otto, *Fools Are Everywhere: The Court Jester around the World* (Chicago: University of Chicago Press, 2001), 48.

4. Kings like Henry VIII used to have multiple "grooms of the stool," servants who literally wiped their posteriors and took care of the privy. Politicians today have similar attendants, known commonly as sycophants or "brown-nosers." Because servants of this station weren't seen as whole persons, eighteenth-century noble ladies disrobed in front of them without a second thought.

5. Clive Aslet, *An Exuberant Catalogue of Dreams* (London: Aurum Press, 2013).

6. Marco Pasanella, "Taming Spaces: Living Large," *New York Times,* February 17, 2005, http://www.nytimes.com/2005/02/17/garden /17room.html?_r=0.

7. Paul Ginsborg, *The Politics of Everyday Life,* 113.

8. "Stay Safe, Stay Indoors," *The Economist,* February 22, 2014, 27.

9. According to Jewish tradition, there are 613 seeds in a fully mature pomegranate—the number of laws God gave Israel.

10. Blaise Pascal, *Pensées* (1958; Project Gutenberg, 2006), chap. 430, p. 118, http://gutenberg.org/files/18269/18269-h/18269-h.htm.

11. Timothy Radcliffe, *Take the Plunge* (London: Burns and Oates, 2012), 109.

12. I borrow the metaphor of conversation as "hot air" from Adam Gopnik, *The Table Comes First* (New York: Vintage, 2012), 189.

13. Bill McKibben calls the spice and olive oil exemption to localism the "Marco Polo Exemption."

14. John Wesley, in correspondence with Francis Asbury, 1788.

15. Anyone who has ever seen one of the many exposés of factory farms and their nightmarish treatment of animals knows that Community-Supported Agriculture (CSA) is more than "elitist diner clubs for lefties." Christian tables need to embrace forms of locavorism, farmers' markets, kitchen-gardening, and especially the eating of "ethically raised" animals.

CHAPTER 5: SETTING THE TABLE AT CHURCH

1. Robert J. Karris, *Eating Your Way through Luke's Gospel* (St. Joseph, MN: Liturgical Press, 2006), 56.

2. Johann Wolfgang von Goethe, *Observations on Leonardo da Vinci's Celebrated Painting of the Last Supper* (1821), https://archive.org /details/observationsonloonoehgoog.

3. For an excellent discussion of the painting, see Leo Steinberg, *Leonardo's Incessant Last Supper* (New York: MIT Press, 2001).

4. John Calvin, *Institutes of the Christian Religion*, IV.xvii.3.

5. Augustine, *Confessions*, VII.x.16.

6. Russell E. Richey, "Family Meal, Holy Communion, and Love Feast: Three Ecumenical Metaphors," in *Ecumenical and Interreligious Perspectives* (Nashville: Quarterly Review of Books, 1992), 17–29.

7. John Calvin, *Institutes of the Christian Religion*, IV.xvii.7.

8. Thomas Aquinas, *Summa Theologica*, IIIa, q80, a6. He goes on to quote Augustine in reference to 1 Corinthians 5:11: "We cannot inhibit any person from Communion, except he has openly confessed or has been named and convinced by some ecclesiastical or lay tribunal."

9. Gerard Manley Hopkins, "Pied Beauty," http://www.bartleby.com /122/13.html.

10. See "Hunger Strikes," *The Economist*, April 19, 2014, 74.

11. Virgil, "Moretum," lines 103–104, *The Works of Virgil*, trans. John Augustine Wilstach (Boston: Houghton Mifflin, 1884), vol. 1, 123. See Adam Gopnik, *The Table Comes First* (New York: Vintage, 2012). The phrase also appears in Augustine's *Confessions*.

12. Bernard MacLaverty, introduction to his *Collected Stories* (London: Random House, 2014).

13. Lars Rood, personal conversation with the author.

CHAPTER 6: SETTING THE TABLE IN THE WORLD

1. Gordon W. Allport, "A Psychological Approach to the Study of Love and Hate," in *Explorations in Altruistic Love and Behavior*, ed. Pitirim A. Sorokin (Boston: Beacon Press, 1950), 160.

2. John Horsch (1867–1941), historian of the Mennonite Church, tells this story. It is found in Myron S. Augsburger, *The Expanded Life: The Sermon on the Mount for Today* (Nashville: Abingdon, 1972), 54–55.

3. See the HBO special *Magic and Bird: A Courtship of Rivals*, https://www.youtube.com/watch?v=jtykEHPRO1Q. Pick up the program at 52:22, ending at 55:02.

4. Terry Walker, "The Will to Whimsy," *Times Literary Supplement*, June 3, 1994, 11.

5. Adam Gopnik, *The Table Comes First* (New York: Vintage, 2012), 230.

6. Alain de Botton, "The Art of a Lively Conversation," *Utne Reader*, March–April 2009, http://www.utne.com/mind-and-body/the-art-of-a-lively-conversation.aspx#axzz3BR6yq4ag.

7. John T. Edge, "The Lunch Counter," *Garden and Gun*, June/July 2014, 82.

CONCLUSION

1. "Johnny Cash - Supper Time," YouTube video, 2:54, posted by "johnnycashfanuk," February 13, 2010, http://www.youtube.com/watch?v=PsM7TiDcnko.

ABOUT THE AUTHOR

 A leading figure in bridging scholarship, pop culture, and the church, LEONARD SWEET holds the E. Stanley Jones chair at Drew University, serves as the distinguished visiting professor at Tabor College, and is a visiting distinguished professor at George Fox University. Founder and president of SpiritVenture Ministries, he is a popular speaker and the chief writer for sermons.com. Sweet has written numerous books, including *The Well-Played Life*, *SoulTsunami*, and *Carpe Mañana*. He is regularly listed among the most influential Christians in the United States. Learn more and keep up with Leonard on Facebook, on Twitter, and at leonardsweet.com.